Past, Present & Personal

Past, Present & Personal

TEACHING WRITING IN U.S. HISTORY

WILLIAM C. KASHATUS
Foreword by Gary B. Nash

HEINEMANN
Portsmouth, NH

Heinemann

A division of Reed Elsevier Ir
361 Hanover Street
Portsmouth, NH 03801–391
www.heinemann.com

Offices and agents throughout

© 2002 by William C. Kasha

The author and publisher wish to thank those who have generously given permission to reprint borrowed material:

Excerpts from "The Friends Public School During the American Revolution" by Justin Pertschuk are reprinted by permission from *The Concord Review* (Volume 6, Number 1), Fall 1994. Permission granted by Will Fitzhugh, Editor, *The Concord Review.*

Excerpts from "I Have A Dream" by Martin Luther King, Jr. are reprinted by arrangement with the Estate of Martin Luther King Jr., care of Writers House as agent for the proprietor, New York, NY. Copyright © 1963 by Dr. Martin Luther King Jr., copyright renewed 1991 by Coretta Scott King.

Excerpts from "A Young Voice on Voluntarism: Could I handle it? Was it worth it?" by Alexis Bodenheimer, *The Philadelphia Inquirer*, April 20, 1997. Permission granted by *The Philadelphia Inquirer.*

Photographs from *Dick Clark's American Bandstand* by Dick Clark and Fred Bronson. Copyright 1997 by Harper Collins, New York, pp. 52–53, 56–57, 112–113. Permission granted by Dick Clark Productions Inc.

Photograph, "Rooftop Squatters Opposite Shibe Park," taken October 1929. Permission granted by Urban Archives, Temple University, Philadelphia, PA.

Cartoon, "The World's Constable" by Louis Dalrymple, *Judge Magazine*, January 7, 1905. Permission granted by The Granger Collection Ltd., New York, NY.

Photograph, "Frederick Douglass" by unknown daguerreotypist, 1848. Permission granted by Chester County Historical Society, West Chester, PA.

Photograph, "Galusha Pennypacker" by T. W. Taylor, 1861. Permission granted by Chester County Historical Society, West Chester, PA.

Photograph, "William Kashatus in Living History," by Joel Zarska. *Chester County Town & Country Living*, Spring 2000, p. 28. Permission granted by Joel Zarska Productions, Stony Creek Mills, PA.

Library of Congress Cataloging-in-Publication Data

Kashatus, William C., 1959–
   Past, present, and personal: teaching writing in U.S. history / William C. Kashatus.
     p. cm.
Includes bibliographical references.
  ISBN 0-325-00449-8 (alk. paper)
   1. United States—History—Study and teaching.   2. United States—History—Research.
3. United States—Historiography.   4. Historiography—Study and teaching—United States.
5. Portfolios in education—United States.   I. Title: Past, present, and personal.   II. Title.
E175.8 .K266   2002
973′.07′2—dc21   2002005952

Editor: Danny Miller
Production service: bookworks
Production coordinator: Lynne Reed
Cover design: Joni Doherty
Cover photograph: "Syng Inkstand" used courtesy of the National Park Service Independence National Historical Park—Library, Philadelphia, PA.
Typesetter: TechBooks
Manufacturing: Steve Bernier

Printed in the United States of America on acid-free paper
06 05 04 03 02 DA 1 2 3 4 5

For John Grace, Mark Franek, and Jonathan Kulp,
master teachers, and dear friends

Contents

Foreword

I didn't like history very much in high school, but I did like writing. It began with a junior high school teacher who read short items aloud from *The New Yorker*'s "Talk of the Town" and then got us to write one-page essays on everyday objects or events—noses, pickles, lamp shades, the weather, a car crash, anything at all. Not that we liked it; at least at first. But our teacher planted the seed. He showed us how to construct a sentence, a paragraph, a short essay. He got us thinking about words—their fascinating variety, where they came from, how their meanings differed, how much fun it was to learn new words and use them. In time, this business of putting words together grew on me. Writing for the sports page of the high school newspaper turned out to be a lot more fun than studying history. In our history class, we didn't write much. We studied our textbook, learned the facts, memorized the dates, took quizzes (usually multiple choice), and, occasionally, wrote short definitions of this or that—the Navigation Acts, the Missouri Compromise, the Underwood Tariff, the Zimmermann Note. None of this had much flesh and blood in it. Why we should care to learn about all these facts and dates wasn't clear. Hence, I associated writing with literature and journalism, not with history.

That would all change in college when I discovered that history was literature—literature of a different kind. And writing about history was a completely new experience. Our professors assumed, contrary to the belief of my high school teacher, that we might have something to say about history, even if it was a small deviation from what we found in the textbook or in assigned monographs. Such an exhilarating—and daunting–thought! In producing a short report on a particular book, we were expected to show a grain of independent thinking and to express ourselves in serviceable prose. Then, in producing a term paper, we had to learn about asking a key question or two around which to organize the essay, about doing research, and about formulating an argument. A whole new world was opening up, driven by the powerful notion that everybody could be an historian, something akin to the Quaker notion that the "inward light" resides within every human breast.

Bill Kashatus' book on teaching how to write in high school courses on United States history shows that he has accomplished with sixteen- and seventeen-year-old students what those of my generation in public schools did not do until reaching college. He understands that many teachers, particularly in public schools, will regard his strategies and tactics for cultivating research and writing capabilities as noble, worthy, but unachievable. But he is right that what he has accomplished in private school settings is possible almost everywhere. Today, in the Whittier Union High School District, east of Los Angeles (heavily populated by Latino students), every senior is required to undertake a project leading to a research-based paper. Not all are about history, but all require learning how to research a topic and write coherently about it. The requirement was installed six years ago to combat "senioritis"— the common affliction that turns about-to-graduate eighteen year olds into apathetic learners, just before they are preparing to enter college. Before graduating, each Whittier Union High School District student must stand before a panel of community and faculty members to report the findings of his or her project. Last year, the National Commission on the High School Senior Year produced a report, "Raising Our Sights: No High School Student Left Behind," that recommended that every senior in the nation's high schools complete a written, capstone project.

This book by Bill Kashatus provides precise blueprints for teaching teenagers to write in U. S. history classes. It does so with spirit, self-criticism, imagination, and good humor. Above all, the book can inspire teachers to bring their classrooms alive by convincing students, as he says, "that they, too, have a personal relationship with history; that they are part of a much larger legacy handed down to them from generations of others who came before them."

Gary B. Nash, Director
National Center for History in the Schools,
University of California, Los Angeles

Prologue

In all the years I've known him, Bill Kashatus has always been an incorrigible writer. The author of several books on topics ranging from baseball to biography, Bill, it turns out, was never a natural-born writer as I'd assumed. He was visual, not verbal, by native bent. He had to learn how to write by a visual diagram. And to me that makes all the difference.

No wonder I worried as I began reading this book, that I would think Bill right but irrelevant on every essential point. It didn't matter that students will learn history best by doing it and do it best by writing it. Nor did it matter that students who write will find history more interesting and personally engaging than those who don't, and that such students will acquire a vivifying sense of ownership of their work. It didn't matter because this would be a book only for the few who already took for granted, as Bill does, the rewards of writing history. I should have known better.

It is a truism among baseball buffs like Bill that great managers were rarely great players. The game never came easily to them as it did to more naturally talented players. They had to observe more attentively and think more sharply about things that more gifted teammates scarcely thought about at all. Similarly, Bill, a gifted teacher, had to learn his craft and ponder earnestly all the while about what he was learning. He does not write to display his brilliance, but rather to share what he has learned, and what he has tested in years of classroom teaching.

Past, Present, and Personal is premised on the conviction that writing history is "a learned skill that takes time to develop." As the reader is guided through a year in Bill's American History class, he shows us how we can help students learn that skill. Tracing the unfolding experiences of his students' skills, and imaginations over the course of that year, Bill offers us guidance on the uses of time as patient as it is impassioned, as sensible as it is inspired. As he takes us along with him and his students, he enables us to learn what he has learned. He does not try to distill that knowledge into a few simple rules. He does not pontificate on abstract principles. He does much better. He tells revelatory tales of his travails and triumphs. He lets us see what he is driving at as he devises lesson plans, lets us share his thinking as he sets research assignments, lets us look over his shoulder as he grades papers. But he also allows us to relish the happy surprises and revel in the unpredictability of it all.

Bill does not provide a blueprint for teaching historical writing (which is to say, for teaching students to think for themselves) because there is no blueprint. But despite himself, he teaches us. In gritty detail and in telling anecdotes, he shows us how he has helped his youngsters to be more curious, to connect their curiosity to their own lives, and to think more keenly about both curiosity and their own lives.

No one has ever written so helpfully, or so hopefully, about what actually transpires between teachers and students in the classroom and beyond it. Bill burns to enable his students to lead better, more examined lives. He has written this remarkable book to allow the rest of us to warm ourselves at the fire he has kindled.

Michael Zuckerman
University of Pennsylvania
Philadelphia, PA
Winter 2002

Acknowledgments

*P*ast, Present, and Personal is a book that began more than a decade
ago when I was a graduate student at the University of Pennsylvania.
There I met John Grace, a teacher of history at LaSalle College High
School, who would over the years become a valued colleague and close friend.
Without his support I would not have a doctorate.

Jonathan Kulp of the Episcopal Academy cultivated my teaching abilities,
encouraged my professional development, and supported my ambitions. I will
always be grateful to him for teaching me to strive for excellence rather than
perfection in my career.

I am also extremely grateful to Mark Franek, a teacher of English at the
William Penn Charter School, who helped to shape the way I think about
teaching and writing. Without our exchange of ideas, this book would not
have come to fruition.

I feel honored to have been a teacher at Penn Charter, a school that will
always hold a very special place in my heart. I am grateful to headmaster Earl
Ball for giving me the opportunity to teach there, and to Ed Marks, chair
of the history department, for supporting my writing curriculum. Above all,
I am grateful to the students whose work is contained in this book: Dallas
Alexander, Meghan Baran, Alexis Bodenheimer, Kate Ginty, Dana Greenspon,
Dan Greenberg, Matt Huntington, Katherine Park, Justin Pertschuk, Jesse
Rendell, and Lenee Voss. They taught me so much more than they will ever
know.

Special thanks is due to Gary B. Nash for his insightful foreword and
to Michael Zuckerman for his generous prologue; Will Fitzhugh, editor of
The Concord Review for permission to reprint excerpts of "The Friends Public
School: A Quaker Institution in War"; Writers House, to reprint excerpts of the
"I Have A Dream Speech"; the Chester County Historical Society, Dick Clark,
Ann Kessler, the Library of Congress, the Urban Archives of Temple University,
the Granger Collection, and Joel Zarska, for permission to reprint photographs
from their collections. I am also grateful to Bill Varner of Heinemann for taking

a risk on this book, and Danny Miller for his valuable editorial assistance and personal affirmation of my teaching methods.

Finally, I am grateful to my family—my wife Jackie, and my sons, Tim, Peter, and Ben. Not only have they given me their unconditional love and support, but surrendered a lot of family time in order for me to complete this book. For all of these gifts I am eternally grateful.

Introduction

During my junior year at Earlham College, a history professor encouraged me to depart from the traditional research paper and write a short story on the Underground Railroad. While the content had to be based on documented sources, the style and interpretation could take the form of a narrative account. It was the most challenging, as well as creative and enjoyable, piece of writing that I had ever done as a student. The supreme compliment came a few weeks later when she handed back my essay calling it, "Micheneresque."

While millions will remember James Michener for his award-winning novels such as *Tales of the South Pacific, Hawaii, Centennial, Chesapeake, Poland,* and *The Covenant,* I viewed him as a role model. He, too, attended a Quaker college and went on to begin his career as a high school humanities teacher, just as I was planning to do.

At my professor's suggestion I sent my essay to the Pulitzer Prize–winning novelist, hoping for a response. To my pleasant surprise, I received a reply a week later. "You can write," began the letter. "For sheer skill, you're ahead of where I was at your age. If you continue to work at it, you just might have a good book in you some day."

Two decades later, I continue to be inspired by those first words of encouragement. They have seen me through some pretty tough writer's blocks, and they have stimulated many commentaries, reflective essays, popular history articles, and ten books on various topics ranging from Quakerism and American history, to baseball and biography.

Writing has become, over the years, a passionate form of personal expression that allows me to feel whole, even if my work isn't read by another soul. It has also become a valuable teaching tool to move my students beyond the dry, vocabulary-controlled history text so that they can see the past as something vitally and intrinsically interesting as well as relevant to their own lives.

This book is about how to teach writing in the United States history curriculum. I hope it will inspire high school teachers to challenge themselves as well as their students by suggesting some creative ways to approach the

1

writing process in a discipline that has long been criticized for its regimented and unimaginative nature.

Recently, professional historians and educators concerned about the inadequacy, both in quality and quantity, of history taught in the American high school have emphasized the need for more writing in the curriculum. Not only is this reform "essential to develop critical thinking and reading skills," but also "indispensable for developing the kind of knowledge and habits of mind needed in the education of citizens in a democracy."[1] Some historians have gone so far as to detail the kind of practical knowledge students should be able to demonstrate. Among the most essential areas are:

Chronological thinking, or developing a clear sense of historical time, past, present, and future in order to explain "historical succession and duration, continuity and change."

Historical comprehension, including the ability to "read historical narratives" and to "describe the past through the eyes and experiences of those who were there, as revealed through their writings and artifacts," and to avoid "present-mindedness," or imposing contemporary values and moral conventions on the past.

Historical analysis and interpretation, including the ability to "compare and contrast the experiences, beliefs and motives" of people from a diversity of social and economic backgrounds as well as to "analyze how these differing motives and beliefs shaped their behavior." Also, to compare and evaluate "competing historical explanations of the past."

Historical research, or the ability to develop historical questions from one's own study of historical documents, photographs, and artifacts as well as to judge the credibility of those sources.

Historical issues-analysis and decision-making, or the ability to identify problems that "confronted people in the past"; to evaluate the various interests, motives and actions of those people; to arrive at "alternative methods for dealing with their problems"; to analyze whether the decisions they made were good ones and why; and, finally, to take that understanding and "apply it to informed decision-making in the present."[2]

Although the professionals stopped short of recommending a specific writing curriculum for history education, their suggestions urged me to consider the need for on-going writing as a criterion of evaluation of student progress in the above-mentioned areas. In effect, they convinced me that "doing history" is inextricably tied to "writing history."

Doing history by writing it can also be one of the most meaningful—and productive—ways of measuring student progress. Too often, student progress is measured by how well the individual can memorize facts, dates, and events, from a dry, vocabulary-controlled text and, then, regurgitate that information on a test. But that approach fails to address the multiple intelligences of the student.[3] The gifted history teacher will make an earnest effort to address as many of these intelligences as possible so a student's abilities and interests might be tied to his or her development as a writer. Only by tapping into a student's particular interests, abilities, and intelligences can the teacher respect individual differences, cultivate intellectual curiosity in the subject, and provide for student success in writing.

For example, one of the most insightful research papers I read in my fifteen years of teaching high school juniors came from a student-athlete who had an all-consuming interest in baseball. He was, by his own admission, "not a very good writer" or "very interested in history" for that matter. Not surprisingly, he dreaded the thought of having to write a research paper until I suggested that he explore the significance of Shibe Park, one of Philadelphia's early ballparks, to the city's history. Then he jumped at the opportunity, interviewing long-time baseball fans, former players, and employees of the park. Together with the research he completed using newspaper accounts, old photographs, and two books that had been published on the subject, the student wrote an extremely insightful essay. He argued that Shibe was a gathering place for the ethnically diverse peoples of Philadelphia and one that helped them assimilate into American society by learning about the national pastime. The paper was a successful experience for the student because it allowed him to explore a subject that, by nature, was of a strong personal interest to him. He was also a visually oriented and kinesthetic learner who excelled at research, which permitted him to conduct oral history interviews, visit the site of the old ball park, and study photographs of it. By doing so, he gained a better appreciation for writing as a craft and one that is based on process, that is, practiced over a prolonged period of time.

Research, the first step in that process, requires the identification, analysis, and interpretation of historical materials such as documents, photographs, artifacts, and/or oral history. *Research* is another word for "information gathering." It can involve something as simple as background reading in the textbook, combing through general histories on a particular topic, or visiting an historical site and interviewing the tour guide. Information gathering can also be more complex, especially for longer assignments such as the term paper or local history research paper, which not only involves the gathering primary source documents at a special collections institution, but a critical analysis of those documents in order to determine their importance to the topic.

Organization, the second step in the process, requires categorizing and rethinking the information that has been gathered. As the process unfolds, an outline, divided by general headings and more specific subheadings, can be extremely helpful. Not only is this type of outline helpful for a timed in-class test essay, but also for a longer research paper that will be completed over the course of several weeks. The most effective organization provides the writer with a road map, or a clear direction of the essay as well as coherence in the writing process.

Writing is simply a final step. Because writing involves constant refining in order to present the research in a manner that will engage the reader, most students consider it the most difficult stage of the process. Not only must the argument be persuasive, but truly good writing is also creative, reflecting an active historical imagination. That doesn't mean writing fiction or some kind of free-floating self-expression, but rather a creative ability to reconstruct the past through a responsible use of the documentation gathered. Just as important is writing in a manner that respects the past on its own terms, rather than to impose contemporary liberal values and moral conventions on people who lived more than a century or more ago.

Past, Present, and Personal offers one model of how to teach writing in the United States history curriculum. The book is organized into three parts, each of which addresses a particular type of writing. Part One, titled "Past History," explores student interpretation of documents, photographs, and cartoons from the past as well as assessment of that work, and exercises to help develop interpretive skills. Part Two examines present history, or the more traditional forms of writing completed in history class, such as the position paper and the semester-long research paper. I refer to these forms as "present history," because they are contemporary interpretations of past events. I have found that most students choose topics based on their curiosity for the current implications of an historical event, or an interest in examining the antecedents of a current event or interest. Students' works as well as assessment and procedural methods are also provided in this section. Part Three, titled "Personal History," offers suggestions on how to create a "living history classroom" through simulation exercises and activities that will allow students to make a personal connection to the past. It also examines more creative genres of writing such as playwriting and journal-keeping. Again, student work is highlighted along with assessment of that work.

All three of these forms—interpretive, research-based, and experiential—are inter-related and, therefore, form the basis of a writing curriculum in history throughout the school year. Not only do students learn interpretive, research, and experiential techniques in each one, but they learn how to transfer those skills across more traditional as well as creative forms of writing. While this process often begins in the middle school years, it is better suited to high school students, especially sophomores and juniors, who have developed more intellectually to take on the challenges offered in this book. Accordingly, the student work highlighted here comes from the labors of juniors I taught at the William Penn Charter School in Philadelphia, PA. Some excelled at the more traditional forms of writing, having an eye for detail, fact, and a strong motivation for doing research. Others were more reflective, tending to excel at the interpretive aspects of writing. Still others possessed a genuine interest in history, which allowed them to grow as writers in the discipline. There were even those students who did not have a strong interest in the subject, but were still able to develop as writers because of a strong personal interest in the topics on which they chose to write.

Penn Charter is a *private* school. But that should not discourage public or parochial school teachers from applying the writing skills and techniques given in this book. While Penn Charter enjoys a long-standing and fine academic reputation—being founded in 1689 by William Penn, the colonial proprietor of Pennsylvania—the school is more respected today because of its social and economic diversity. Students from affluent as well as middle-class and extremely modest backgrounds attend the school. The average class size is just under 20 students. While there are advanced placement classes, the majority of students are not tracked. Nor did I teach this writing curriculum in an AP course—ever. Each year I requested that the administration give me those students who were the least motivated. Although I always ended up with a mix of motivational and learning styles, I can honestly say that I taught a cross-section of students, much as would be found in a good public or parochial school.

Because Penn Charter is located in Philadelphia, the subject matter examined in this book addresses the social, political, economic, and cultural history of that city or the surrounding region. Readers will appreciate the fact that Philadelphia possesses a rich as well as unique past because of its close association with the early history of the United States itself. But they will also find that the suggestions, exercises, and pedagogy can be easily transferred to their own classrooms, regardless of where they teach.

Having said all that, I wish you good reading and much fulfillment as you look ever forward to the past!

Endnotes

1. Bernard Bailyn, *On the Teaching & Writing of History* (Hanover, NH: University Press of New England, 1994); and The Bradley Commission on History in Schools, *Historical Literacy: The Case for History in American Education*, edited by Paul Gagnon.

(Boston: Houghton Mifflin Company, 1989). The Bradley Commission was created in response to the 1983 report "A Nation at Risk," published by the National Commission on Excellence in Education, which argued that "the very future of the republic is being threatened by the rising tide of mediocrity in high school classrooms."

2. Charlotte Crabtree and Gary B. Nash, *National Standards for United States History* (Los Angeles: University of California/National Center for History in the Schools, 1994), 7.

3. See Howard Gardner, *Frames of Mind: The Theory of Multiple Intelligences* (New York: Basic Books, 1993). According to Gardner, students possess multiple intelligences that include: (1) *Bodily-Kinesthetic,* or using one's body, or part of it, to solve problems and communicate. These students are highly coordinated, often tactile, and enjoy touching things. They are usually good athletes, who would rather participate than spectate; (2) *Intrapersonal,* or being sensitive to one's inner feelings, knowing one's own strengths and weaknesses. These students often keep journals or diaries and enjoy solitude. Sometimes they have an especially refined understanding of how they learn; (3) *Interpersonal,* or being sensitive to and understanding others. Students with a strong interpersonal intelligences will work well with a group and often assume leadership roles; (4) *Logical-Mathematical,* or having the ability to distinguish patterns and approach situations in a logical fashion. These students tend to be precise and methodical, demonstrating the ability to calculate well and excel in scientific activities; (5) *Musical,* or being sensitive to nonverbal sounds in the environment such as rhythms, pitch, and tonal patterns. Students with strong musical intelligence can easily turn sounds into rhythms and have a knack for remembering melodies; and (6) *Spatial,* or having the ability to form a mental model and to be able to maneuver and operate using that model. These students tend to visualize well and think in images and pictures. They excel at representative drawings. These intelligences are not mutually exclusive. Each individual possesses multiple ones in some degree.

Part One: Past History

Teaching with Documents

A history textbook is a wonderful starting place for students in their study of American history. It is a readily available reference source that, in most cases, represents a collection of the most widely accepted historical interpretations, or *historiography,* in the field. If the text has some nice color photographs, tables, and maps with informative captions, the visual learner may not even have to do much reading at all! However, the history textbook alone is not sufficient in teaching the subject. Documents are the "real stuff" of history, and must be carefully integrated into the curriculum.

Distinguishing Between Primary and Secondary Sources

A primary source document is any document created by those who participated in or witnessed the events of the past. Newspapers, journals, diaries, government papers, wills, inventories, speeches, letters, maps, drawings, and photographs are all examples of primary source documents. They convey the past to us in an insightful way that even the best-written article or book cannot do. Documents fascinate students because they are real and they are personal. Using them allows students to directly touch the lives of people in the past. Primary sources sometimes evoke emotional responses, enabling students to see and identify with the human factor in history, including the risks, frailties, courage, and contradictions of those who shaped the past. As students read eyewitness accounts of the Trail of Tears in which the Cherokee nation was forced off their native land, or letters written by common citizens to President Franklin D. Roosevelt expressing concern about the day-to-day hardships they were experiencing during the Great Depression, or look at photographs from the Civil War, they become aware of the deeply human quality as well as subjectivity of history. At the same time it is important for students to realize that primary sources are not the final word, or even the most accurate account, on any given subject. Primary sources reflect the personal, social, political, and/or economic views of the participants, who had their own biases and motives for recording their thoughts. Accordingly, these records challenge students to examine their own biases, created by their own personal circumstances and the social environments in which they live. Ultimately, students come to realize that history is interpretation and that interpreting documents helps them analyze and evaluate contemporary sources, whether they are newspaper accounts, popular magazines, television or radio programs, or Internet sources.

Articles and books, on the other hand, are considered secondary sources written after an historical event, usually ten or more years afterwards. Secondary sources are written to describe, analyze, or reconstruct an earlier event. By their very nature, they are secondhand interpretations, subject to the distortions of time that has elapsed. That doesn't mean they are not useful. Because secondary sources are written years after an historical event, they can provide an extremely helpful perspective and important insight on people, places, and events of the past. In other words, sufficient distance from an historical event affords the contemporary writer a special advantage: he or she can craft his or her own interpretation knowing the effects a particular event or person had on subsequent generations. For example, Arthur M. Schlesinger, Jr.'s *The Age of Jackson* is a Pulitzer-prize-winning interpretation of America during the period 1828 to 1850. Based on a thorough interpretation of primary documents, including newspapers, pamphlets, and the personal papers of some of the most prominent personalities of the Jacksonian era, as well as other respected secondary interpretations, Schlesinger's work offers readers a remarkable perspective of the political, social, economic, and cultural history of America during the antebellum period. Thus, the book has been recognized by two generations of historians as an essential foundation upon which to build their own interpretations of that time period. But had the book been written during the antebellum period, or even during the late nineteenth century, the quality would have been lessened by the fact that there was very little perspective on how the subsequent history had been shaped by those events and, hence, why the Jacksonian period was important at all in the broader landscape of American history.

Often I will begin my history course with an exercise that helps students to recognize primary sources and to distinguish them from secondary sources. I ask them to identify each of the following sources as either a primary source (*p*) or a secondary source (*s*) and then we review their answers:

1. A photograph of the 1927 New York Yankees (p)
2. Copy of the Declaration of Independence in your text (p)
3. A new book about the War of 1812 (s)
4. Your father's high school yearbook (s)
5. A recent newspaper article on the 1848 Seneca Falls Convention (s)
6. Your first-grade report card (s)
7. Tourist's map of the Gettysburg battlefield (s)
8. Tape recording of a speech made by President Richard Nixon (p)

The photograph of the 1927 New York Yankees baseball team is a primary source because it captures the likenesses of the players as they appeared in that year. It doesn't matter if the photo was reproduced from a recently made negative or not; the image itself is the primary source. The copy of the Declaration of Independence is also a primary source because the words were written in 1776 by Thomas Jefferson, the historical actor in this case. Similarly, the tape recording of President Nixon's speech is a primary source because it captures his voice at a specific point in history.

The new book on the War of 1812, the recent newspaper article on the 1848 Seneca Falls Conference, and the tourist's map of the Gettysburg battlefield are all secondary sources, created well after the historical event and by a person who did not participate in the historic event.

Your father's high school yearbook and your first-grade report card are more problematic. On one hand, they very well may represent a primary source if the subject of study is your father or yourself. In that case, your father or you become the historical actor because you've experienced the events that are being researched. On the other hand, most historians would dismiss these as secondary sources since they were created within the last forty years, a time span commonly acknowledged as "contemporary," or too recent for historical analysis.

As you can see, analyzing primary source documents can be tricky. But it's also a valuable exercise for building critical thinking skills and provides students with an essential research tool for writing. They will need this skill to write their local history research paper later in the school year.

A Model for Analyzing Primary Source Documents

I require each student to complete, as a written assignment, a total of six document analyses over the span of the course. Several more documents are completed as cooperative learning exercises in class and for a local history research project. Some were written by the most prominent figures in American history.

Others, were written by lesser-known personalities. Authors included males and females, whites, African Americans and Native Americans, and dealt with a variety of topics ranging from politics to social theory. Collectively, the selection and content of these sources give students an important understanding of the diversity of our nation. It is a subjective list, consisting of those primary sources that are most often contained in supplementary readings for both high school texts and college survey courses. There are a total of just thirty two documents.[1] While some teachers may think the number too few, I have found that the average student will become overwhelmed if asked to do more rather than less. Besides, most textbooks or editorial commentary tend to summarize the argument for the student. By limiting the number of primary source documents to thirty two, I register the importance of the sources with students and require that they make a serious effort to engage them: to ask probing questions and to find answers for themselves; to develop the critical thinking skills that allows them to determine the author's bias; and to understand the significance of each document to their study of American history.

The questions I ask students to address range from basic identification to issues that require more critical thinking:

> **What?** What kind of document is it? What is the content? The answers to these questions may seem obvious, but the way students describe the documents actually indicates their understanding of it. The object here is to summarize the important issues raised in the document and describe the nature of the document itself: a newspaper account, personal letter, government transcript, and so on.

> **Who?** Who is the author of the document? Students may not always be able to identify the author by name. Sometimes a document makes no reference to a particular person. In this case, the student must try to identify other characteristics such as gender, race, ethnicity, political, or religious affiliation. These characteristics may very well prove to be important in understanding the author's motive for writing the document.

> **When?** When was the document written? Students should not only be able to identify the date, but major events that were occurring at the time. This identification is extremely important to understanding the historical context of the document. For example, a student must know that Harriet Beecher Stowe's work, *Uncle Tom's Cabin* (1852), was written shortly after the passage of the Fugitive Slave Act in 1850. Without that knowledge, her book becomes irrelevant because it was written in response to that act. Its immediate popularity among abolitionists and controversy among slaveholders prompted President

Lincoln, when he later met Stowe, to remark: "So, you're the person whose book started this great [Civil] war!"

Where? Where was the document written? The location may or may not be significant. Thomas Paine's authorship of *Common Sense* could have been written anywhere in the colonies in 1776 and still would have mobilized the American people for independence from Great Britain. On the other hand, Lincoln's *Gettysburg Address* (1863) was delivered near a central Pennsylvania battlefield where hundreds of Union soldiers lost their lives. The fact that Lincoln was there to dedicate a cemetery to those men, as well as the fact that he honored the sacrifice they made, has a profound significance in terms of the content and emotional impact of the speech.

Why? Why did the author write the document? The question of motive is the most difficult one to answer. In an edited collection of documents, there is often an explanation of motive preceding the document. However, if students have done their homework and understand the historical context of the document as well as the background of its author, they can often make an educated guess as to the motive.

So what? This is another way of asking, "Why is the document important in the broader context of American history?" In other words, what is the significance of the document? If the document is not significant to students' subject of study, it should probably not be used in their research paper. In responding to this question students should consider the purpose of the document, what it reveals about a person's opinion or bias, and the conclusions drawn from it.

Analyzing Treatises, Declarations, and Speeches

Below are excerpts of three of the documents I use in the course. Each one is followed by two student analyses and my assessment of them.

DOCUMENT 1: Thomas Paine, *Common Sense*
(Philadelphia, January 1776)

... In the following pages I offer nothing more than simple facts, plain arguments, and common sense.

Volumes have been written on the subject of the struggle between England and America. Men of all ranks have embarked in the controversy, from different motives, and with various designs; but all have been ineffectual, and the period of debate is closed. Arms as the last resource decide the contest;

the appeal was the choice of the King, and the continent has accepted the challenge . . .

The sun never shone on a cause of greater worth. 'Tis not the affair of a city, a county, a province, or a kingdom; but of a continent—of at least one eighth part of the habitable globe. 'Tis not the affair of a day, a year, or an age; posterity are virtually involved in the contest and will be more or less affected even to the end of time by the proceedings now. Now is the seed time of continental union, faith and honor. The least fracture now will be like a name engraved with the point of a pin in the tender bark of a young oak; the wound will enlarge the tree, and posterity will read it in full-grown characters . . .

As much has been said of the advantages of reconciliation, which like an agreeable dream, has passed away and left us as we were; it is but right that we should examine the contrary side of the argument and inquire into some of the many material injuries which these colonies sustain, and always will sustain, by being connected with and dependent on Great Britain . . .

I have heard it asserted by some that as America has flourished under her former connection with Great Britain, the same connection is necessary toward her future happiness, and will always have the same effect. Nothing can be more fallacious than this kind of argument. We may as well assert that because a child has thrived upon milk. It is never to have meat, or that the first twenty years of our lives [are] to become a precedent for the next twenty. But even this is admitting more than is true, for I answer roundly [plainly] that America would have flourished as much, and probably much more, gad no European power taken any notice of her. The commerce by which she has enriched herself are the necessaries of life and will always have a market while eating is the custom in Europe . . .

Alas! We have been long led away by ancient prejudices and [have] made large sacrifices to superstition. We have boasted the protection of Great Britain, without considering that her motive was *interest* not *attachment* and that she did not protect us from *our enemies* on *our account,* but from *her enemies* on *her own account* . . .

. . . France and Spain never were, nor perhaps ever will be, our enemies as Americans, but as . . . subjects of Great Britain.

But Britain is the parent country say some. Then the more shame upon her conduct. Even brutes do not devour their young, nor savages make way upon their families; wherefore, the assertion, if true, turns to her reproach; but it happens not to be true, or only partly so, . . . Europe and not England is the parent country of America. This new world has been the asylum for the persecuted lovers of civil and religious liberty from *every part* of Europe. Hither have they fled, not from the tender embraces of the mother, but from the cruelty of the monster; and it is so far true of England that the same tyranny which drove the first emigrants from home pursues their descendants still . . .

I challenge the warmest advocate for reconciliation to show a single advantage that this continent cap reap by being connected with Great Britain. I repeat the challenge: not a single advantage is derived. Our grain will fetch it's price in any market in Europe and our imported goods must be paid for, buy them where we will . . .

Everything that is right and reasonable pleads for separation. The blood of the slain, the weeping voice of nature cries, 'TIS TIME TO PART. Even the distance at which the Almighty has placed England and America is a strong and natural proof that the authority of the one over the other was never the design of Heaven. The time likewise at which the continent was discovered adds weight to the argument, and the manner in which it was peopled increases the force of it. The Reformation was preceded by the discovery of America, as if the Almighty graciously meant to open a sanctuary to the persecuted in future years, when home should afford neither friendship nor safety . . .

But where, some say is the king of America? I'll tell you, friend: he reigns above, and he does not make havoc of mankind like the Royal Brute of Great Britain. Yet, that we may not appear to be defective even in earthly honors, let a day be solemnly set apart for proclaiming the charter. Let it be brought forth placed on the Divine Law, the Word of God. Let a crown be placed thereon, by which the world may know that so far as we approve of monarchy, in America THE LAW IS KING. For as in absolute governments the king is law, so in free countries the law ought to be king and there ought to be no other . . .

O ye that love mankind! Ye that dare oppose not only the tyranny but the tyrant, stand forth! Every spot of the old world is overrun with oppression. Freedom hath been hunted around the globe. Asia and Africa have expelled her. Europe regards her like a stranger, and England has given her warning to depart. O! Receive the fugitive, and prepare in time an asylum for all mankind . . .

Let the names of Whig and Tory be extinct; and let none other be heard among us, than those of a good citizen, an open and resolute friend, and a virtuous supporter of the RIGHTS OF MANKIND, and of the FREE AND INDEPENDENT STATES OF AMERICA.[2]

STUDENT ANALYSIS 1:

Who: Thomas Paine
When: 1776
Where: Philadelphia
What: Paine thinks that the colonists are losing money in trade and are opening themselves up to wars by being part of the British kingdom.

Why: Paine wants the colonists to revolt against England by declaring their independence.

So what: If Paine hadn't written *Common Sense,* the common people wouldn't have understood the main issues in the conflict with England. They probably would not have separated.

The sparse quality of this student's analysis is typical at the beginning of the school year. Since the course begins with a study of Colonial America and its relationship to Great Britain, *Common Sense* is one of the first documents we read, along with Thomas Jefferson's *Declaration of Independence.* Students do not yet have a solid understanding of my expectations and will generally give only the basic information required. The fact that this particular student retained the list of questions in the analysis underscores this tendency. Nor is the summary of the argument very thorough. Paine's remarks about the benefits of economic prosperity and peace with other nations are the only reasons identified for American independence. In fact, Paine also emphasizes geographic (i.e., "the distance at which the Almighty has placed England and America is a strong and natural proof that the authority of the one over the other was never the design of Heaven"), legalistic (i.e., "in America THE LAW IS KING"), and the tyranny of a religiously intolerant king are also important reasons for separation. While the writing and the mechanics are not as refined as they will become later in the school year, the student does demonstrate a fairly accurate understanding of the argument as well as Paine's motive. Thus, this is an average or "C" level piece of work.

STUDENT ANALYSIS 2:

Thomas Paine was an English immigrant who settled in Philadelphia. He wrote "Common Sense" in January of 1776 in order to convince the common people that they should separate from Great Britain. Paine's pamphlet gave many reasons for American independence. One reason was economic. Paine believed that an independent America would have better trading relations with other European countries. Another reason was having friendly relations with other countries who were enemies of Great Britain. Paine also give two "common sense" arguments. First, he says that the colonies have outgrown England, the parent country, and it's time to separate because they no longer need parents. Then, he says that England and America are so distant from each other that God wanted a separation between the two. "Common Sense" was important because it explained American independence to the common people in terms they could understand. He used references to religion, parents and children, economic theory, all of which could be understood by common people. Paine was also deeply committed to American independence. His words seem to "shout" at the reader from the page. "Common Sense" wasn't meant for the highly-educated politicians who served on the Second Continental Congress. They would have Thomas Jefferson, one of their own members, write a separate declaration six months later.

This student's analysis is more detailed, coherent, and insightful than the previous one. The knowledge gained from the textbook is put to an effective use, allowing the student to place Paine in the broader context of the Revolutionary era by comparing his work to Jefferson's *Declaration of Independence.* She also demonstrates a high level of abstract thinking addressing Paine's rhetorical style—his manipulation of emotionally charged vocabulary, his familial reference to the maturation of colonial society, and the rational, common-sense-like appeal he makes to his readers. Finally, she demonstrates a clear, accurate understanding and significance of Paine's argument. Indeed, many professional historians have credited Paine for successfully mobilizing popular support for the American Revolution.[3] Read aloud in taverns, coffee houses, and homes throughout the English-speaking world, *Common Sense* was the first American "best seller" with more than 120,000 copies sold within the first three months of publication.[4] The 47-page pamphlet catered to the general public by using "plain arguments, simple facts, and common sense" and anticipated Thomas Jefferson's *Declaration of Independence* by more than six months.[5] For all these reasons, this particular analysis earned an "A" grade and was one of the best I have ever received at such an early point in the course. Having said that, I believe the student still could have integrated specific quotations from *Common Sense* into her analysis, thereby demonstrating an even better understanding of Paine's argument.

The next series of excerpts come from *The Declaration of Sentiments,* a major staple of the Jacksonian period. Inspired by the idealism of Jacksonian democracy, Lucretia Mott, Elizabeth Cady Stanton, and other female reformers assembled at the first women's rights convention at Seneca Falls, New York, and adopted this declaration and a series of resolutions. In ringing words that appealed to the principles of the *Declaration of Independence,* they announced their determination to fight for the full rights and privileges of United States citizenship.

DOCUMENT 2: Lucretia Mott and Elizabeth Cady Stanton,
Declaration of Sentiments and Resolutions on Women's Rights
(Seneca Falls, New York, July 19, 1848)

When in the course of human events, it become necessary for one portion of the family of man to assume among the people of the earth a position different from that which they have hitherto occupied, but one to which the laws of nature and of nature's God entitle them, a decent respect to the opinions of mankind requires that they should declare the causes that impel them to such a course.

We hold these truths to be self-evident: that all men and women are created equal; that they are endowed by the Creator with certain inalienable rights; that among these are life, liberty, and the pursuit of happiness; that to secure these rights governments are instituted, deriving their just powers from the consent of the governed. Whenever any form of government becomes destructive of these ends, it is the right of those who suffer from it to refuse allegiance to it, and to insist upon the institution of a new government, laying its foundation on such principles, and organizing its powers in such form, as to them shall seem most likely to effect their safety and happiness . . . But when a long train of abuses and usurpations pursuing invariably the same object evinces a design to reduce them under absolute despotism, it is their duty to throw off such government, and to provide new guards for their future security. Such has been the patient sufferance [suffering] of the women under this government, and such is now the necessity which constrains them to demand the equal station to which they are entitled.

The history of mankind is a history of repeated injuries and usurpations on the part of man toward woman, having in direct object the establishment of an absolute tyranny over her. To prove this, let facts be submitted to a candid world.

Having deprived her of this first right of a citizen, the elective franchise [right to vote], thereby leaving her without representation in the halls of legislation, he has oppressed her.

He has made her, if married, in the eye of the law, civilly dead . . .

Now, in view of this entire disenfranchisement [loss of right to vote] of one half of the people of this country, their social and religious degradation—in view of the unjust laws above mentioned, and because women do feel themselves aggrieved, oppressed, and fraudulently deprived of their most sacred rights, we insist that they have immediate admission to all the rights and privileges which belong to them as citizens of the United States.

In entering upon the great work before us, we anticipate no small amount of misconception, misrepresentation, and ridicule; but we shall use every instrumentality [means] within our power to effect our object. We shall employ agents, circulate tracts, petition the state and national legislatures, and endeavor to enlist the pulpit and the press in our behalf. We hope this convention will be followed by a series of conventions embracing every part of the country.

RESOLUTIONS

Resolved, That all laws which prevent woman from occupying such a station in society as her conscience shall dictate, or which place her in a position inferior to that of man, are contrary to the great precept of nature, and, therefore, of no force or authority.

Resolved, That woman is man's equal—was intended to be so by the Creator, and the highest good of the race demands that she should be recognized as such . . .

Resolved, That woman has too long rested satisfied in the circumscribed [narrow] limits which corrupt customs and a perverted [misdirected] application of the Scriptures have marked out for her, and it is time she should move in the enlarged sphere which her great Creator has assigned her.

Resolved, That it is the duty of the women of this country to secure to themselves their sacred right to the elective franchise.

Resolved, That the equality of human rights results necessarily from the fact of the identity [sameness of essential character] of the race in capabilities and responsibilities.

Resolved, That the speedy success of our cause depends upon the zealous and untiring efforts of both men and women, for the overthrow of the monopoly of the pulpit, and for the securing to women an equal participation with men in the various trades, professions, and commerce.

Resolved, therefore, That, being invested by the Creator with the same capabilities, and the same consciousness of responsibility for their exercise, it is demonstrably the right and duty of woman, equally with man, to promote every righteous cause by every righteous means; and especially in regard to the great subjects of morals and religion, it is self-evidently her right to participate with her brother in teaching them, both in private and in public, by writing and by speaking, by any instrumentalities proper to be used, and in any assemblies proper to be held . . .[6]

STUDENT ANALYSIS 1:

The "Declaration of Sentiments" grew out of the 1848 women's right convention in Seneca Falls, New York. It was written by the convention's organizers, Lucretia Mott and Elizabeth Cady Stanton, to inspire and organize women to fight for civil rights.

The document lists a number of injustices against women. Women, for example, were denied access to professions such as medicine, law and the ministry. If married, they had no property rights. Whatever wages they earned belonged to their husbands. If divorced, a mother had no child custody rights. All of these limitations were wrong since women were every bit as intelligent as men, some even more. Worst of all, women did not have the right to vote. The document is followed by eleven resolutions demanding redress of these grievances. These resolutions state that:

1. Women do not have to follow any law that makes them inferior to men.
2. The Bible should be ignored because it defends the inferior position of women.
3. Women have a duty to fight for the right to vote.
4. Both women and men must fight for the equal rights of women.

The main reason the document was so powerful was because it was modeled after Thomas Jefferson's "Declaration of Independence," with some clear exceptions. Whereas Jefferson write that "all men are created equal," Mott and Stanton wrote that "all men and women are created equal." Jefferson charges the King of England with several injustices. Mott and Stanton say that men are just as bad as the king by charging them with several injustices and playing upon the patriotism of their readers. The significance of this document is that it inspired a future generation of suffrage leaders to push for female voting rights. That goal was realized in 1919 with the passage of the Nineteenth Amendment to the United States Constitution.

Students read *The Declaration of Sentiments* just before or just after the Thanksgiving recess. That means that they've already completed at least two other document analyses and have read—and hopefully thought about—ten of the thirty documents we cover in the course. Naturally, as the school year unfolds and students have had experiences with this type of writing, my own standards of what is acceptable change, becoming more demanding. By the end of the first semester, proper grammar, punctuation, and spelling as well as neatness are nonnegotiable. If there are problems in these areas, the writing is immediately returned to the student for revision. In terms of content, all six questions (i.e., Who? What? When? Where? Why? and So What?) must be addressed. While I am still flexible in evaluating the students' responses to the more abstract questions of Why? and So What?, I do expect that an earnest effort will be made to engage the work.

Evaluating a student's "earnest effort" is a tricky matter. The evaluation should be based not only on the sophistication of the writing, but also an understanding of the student's progress as a writer. I do not, for example, use the grade as a punitive measure. That is why poor spelling and grammar are immediately returned to the student for revision without a grade. On the other hand, I want to encourage my students' growth as writers by showing them that I can see and appreciate their improvement, no matter how small it might be. If all these basic criteria are met, the work deserves a grade in the "C" range, which is "average." If the writing exceeds these criteria, the grade is, of course, higher.

The previous analysis was given a "B." In addition to meeting all the basic criteria, the piece demonstrates a strong understanding of the content, motives, and rhetoric of the document. The student not only lists all the grievances against men but gives a detailed summary of the resolutions. There is a clear understanding that the document was written "to inspire and organize women to fight for civil rights." The student also recognizes that Mott and Stanton used the *Declaration of Independence* as an important rhetorical device for their cause in the hope of "playing upon the patriotism of their readers."

Where the document falls short is in the accuracy of interpretation and its wordiness. While the student's interpretation of the grievance section is very sound, his analysis of the resolutions is less so. For example, the student's interpretation that the "Bible should be ignored because it defends the inferior position of women" is not correct. Mott and Stanton wrote that "a perverted application of the Scriptures" has placed women in a position of inferiority to men and that "it is time she should move in the enlarged sphere which her great Creator has assigned her." In fact, the preceding resolution states: "That woman is man's equal—was intended to be so by the Creator." Similarly, the student's interpretation that "both women and men must fight for the equal rights of women" is not exactly what Mott and Stanton meant when they wrote that "the speedy success of our cause depends on the zealous and untiring efforts of both men and women." Their *Declaration* did not insist that men join their struggle as much as it suggested that a "speedy success" to their cause would have to involve a partnership between the two sexes if "equal participation with men in the various trades, professions, and commerce" were to occur.[7]

Had the student been more concise in his interpretation, he might have even avoided these difficulties. But there is a popular belief that the longer a piece of writing, the better the quality of work, or at least the work reveals an earnest effort on the part of the student to engage the document. Not so. The following student analysis was given an "A" because of exceptional—and concise—engagement.

STUDENT ANALYSIS 2:

"The Declaration of Sentiments" was written by Lucretia Mott and Elizabeth Cady Stanton at the Seneca Falls (New York)Womens' Convention in 1848. Modeled after the "Declaration of Independence," these reformers showed the hypocrisy of patriotic men who believed in treating females as inferiors and asserted that "all men *and women* are created equal." Both Mott and Stanton were Quaker reformers, who believed that men "endeavored in every way to destroy a woman's confidence in her own powers, to lessen her self-respect, and to make her willing to lead a dependent and abject life." They list several ways in which men oppressed women by depriving them of their God-given and "inalienable right" to vote, to hold property, and to have "equal participation with men in the various trades, professions, and commerce." These grievances are followed by a series of resolutions which reveal the reformers' strategy for gaining equal rights. This document was the first in the nation's history to call for the "sacred right to the elective franchise" for women and paved the way for the Nineteenth Amendment of the U.S. Constitution, 72 years later.

The strength of this student's work is in her engagement of the document itself. She demonstrates an exceptional understanding of the work by integrating quotations from the document into her own writing. While not as detailed in her summary of the grievances and resolutions as the previous student, the piece does reflect an accurate interpretation of the various points given in each section of the document. She also addresses all of the necessary questions and does so in a concise manner.

Some readers might be interested in knowing why she identified Mott and Stanton as "Quaker" reformers. Because Penn Charter is a Quaker school, students quickly become familiar with the inferences of that term, which is often equated with liberal reform movements due to the long history of political activism in the Society of Friends. Thus, this student's identification of Mott and Stanton as "Quaker reformers" serves to explain their roles as activists in the women's right movement. At another school, the use of that term should probably be clarified!

DOCUMENT 3: The Reverend Dr. Martin Luther King, Jr.,
The March on Washington Address (The Mall, Washington, D.C., August 28, 1963)

Five score years ago, a great American, in whose symbolic shadow we stand, signed the Emancipation Proclamation. This momentous decree came as a great beacon light of hope to millions of Negro slaves . . .

But one hundred years later, we must face the tragic fact that the Negro is still not free. One hundred years later, the life of the Negro is still sadly crippled by the manacles of segregation and the chains of discrimination. One hundred years later, the Negro lives on an island of poverty in the midst of a vast ocean of material prosperity . . .

When the architects of our republic wrote the magnificent words of the Constitution and the Declaration of Independence, they were signing a promissory note to which every American was to fall heir. This note was a promise that all men would be guaranteed the unalienable rights of life, liberty, and the pursuit of happiness... Instead of honoring this sacred obligation, America has given the Negro people a bad check...

But in the process of gaining our rightful place we must not be guilty of wrongful deeds... We must forever conduct our struggle on the high plane of dignity and discipline. We must not allow our creative protest to degenerate into physical violence... the marvelous new militancy which has engulfed the Negro community must not lead us to a distrust of all white people, for many of our white brothers have come to realize that their freedom is inextricably bound to our freedom. We cannot walk alone.

There are those who are asking the devotees of civil rights, "When will you be satisfied?"

We can never be satisfied as long as the Negro is the victim of the unspeakable horrors of police brutality. We can never be satisfied as long as our bodies, heavy with fatigue of travel, cannot gain lodging in the motels of the highways and the cities...

We can never be satisfied as long as a Negro in Mississippi cannot vote and a Negro in New York believes he has nothing for which to vote...

I say to you today, my friends, that in spite of the difficulties and frustrations of the moment I still have a dream. It is a dream deeply rooted in the American dream. I have a dream that one day this nation will rise up and live out the true meaning of its creed: 'We hold these truths to be self-evident; that all men are created equal.' I have a dream that one day on the red hills of Georgia the sons of former slaves and the sons of former slave holders will be able to sit down together at the table of brotherhood.

I have a dream that one day even the state of Mississippi, a desert state sweltering with the heat of injustice and oppression, will be transformed into an oasis of freedom and justice. I have a dream that my four little children will one day live in a nation where they will not be judged by the color of their skin but by the content of their character. I have a dream that one day the state of Alabama, whose governor's lips are presently dripping with the words of interposition and nullification, will be transformed into a situation where little black boys and black girls will be able to join hands with little white boys and girls and walk together as sisters and brothers...

This will be the day when all of God's children will be able to sing with new meaning, 'My country 'tis of thee, sweet land of liberty, of thee I sing...

And if America is to be a great nation, this must become true. So let freedom ring from the prodigious hilltops of New Hampshire. Let freedom ring from the mighty mountains of New York. Let freedom ring from the heightening Alleghenies of Pennsylvania!

Let freedom ring from the snowcapped Rockies of Colorado. Let freedom ring from the curvaceous peaks of California! But not only that; let freedom ring from Stone Mountain of Tennessee! Let freedom ring from every hill and molehill of Mississippi. From every mountainside, let freedom ring.

When we let freedom ring, when we let it ring from every village and every hamlet, from every state and every city, we will be able to speed up that day when all of God's children, black men and white men, Jews and Gentiles, Protestants and Catholics, will be able to join hands and sing in the words of the old Negro spiritual, 'Free at last! Free at last! Thank God Almighty, we are free at last!' [8]

STUDENT ANALYSIS 1

On August 28, 1963, the Reverend Dr. Martin Luther King Jr., the leader of the Southern Leadership Conference and the most noted civil rights leader in America, stood before the Lincoln Memorial on the Washington D.C. Mall and delivered his "I Have A Dream Speech."

In his speech, King warned that the "whirlwind of revolt" would continue if the civil rights of blacks were denied. "We will not be satisfied," he said, "until justice rolls down like the waters and righteousness like a mighty stream." Then, in the cadence of a southern black preacher, he spoke of his own dream: "I have a dream that some day, in the red hills of Georgia, the sons of former slaves and slave owners will sit together at the table of brotherhood . . . that even Mississippi will become an oasis of freedom and justice . . . that boys and girls of both races will join hands and walk together as sisters and brothers . . . that my four children can live in a nation where they will be judged on the basis of their character and not the color of their skin . . . that all of God's children, black men and white men, Jews and Gentiles, Protestants and Catholics, will be able to join hands and sing in the words of that old Negro spiritual, 'Free at last! Free at last! Thank God Almighty, we are free at last!'

King's speech is considered to be one of the greatest in American history because it called on all Americans to remember that the ideals of justice and equality belong to everyone, regardless of skin color.

Dr. Martin Luther King, Jr.'s moving speech stirred the hearts of more than 200,000 civil rights demonstrators who assembled on the Washington, D.C., Mall in 1963 and continues to inspire students today. I'm still not sure, however, if this particular student was so inspired that he felt obliged to quote all of the most evocative phrases from the speech. Chances are better that after months of hearing my plea to "engage the document by quoting from it," he believed that a block quote would suffice. Not true.

We read the King speech in May, near the end of the school year. By this time, I want students to be able to identify and fragment the most important quotations and integrate them into the body of *their own interpretation.* The problem with the above student's work is that there is very little interpretation of King's words. The quotations are simply placed in the middle of the analysis without any real engagement from the student. While the analysis does address all the basic questions and indicates the significance of the speech, it doesn't go nearly as far as it should. For example, what exactly is the "whirlwind of revolt" to which King refers? What is his position on the use of physical violence in achieving civil rights for black Americans? Why include white people as partners in a dream that involves civil rights for black people? None of these questions are answered and yet the quotations he has chosen beg these very same questions. At this late time in the school year, this document analysis received a "C." The following student analysis leaves no question unanswered.

STUDENT ANALYSIS 2:

On August 28, 1963, the Reverend Dr. Martin Luther King, Jr., a Baptist minister and the most prominent civil rights leader in the nation, brought racial discrimination to the attention of the country when he delivered a highly emotional speech to more than 200,000 demonstrators in Washington, D.C. Known as the "I Have A Dream" speech, King's oration was delivered from the steps of the Lincoln Memorial and began by evoking the example of the Great Emancipator, who freed the slaves. By doing so, King was echoing the same rededication to freedom that Lincoln made at Gettysburg a century earlier.

"But one hundred years later," King insisted, "we must face the tragic fact that the Negro is still not free" because of the "manacles of segregation and the chains of discrimination" he suffers as well as the poverty in which he lives. While he recognized the "new militancy" of younger blacks who had grown impatient for change, he also emphasized that the need for non-violent change as well as joining together with those white people who "have come to realize that their freedom is inextricably bound to our freedom."

Then, addressing the Kennedy administration, which was reluctant to move more forcefully on the issue of civil rights, King said: "There are those who are asking the devotees of civil rights, "When will you be satisfied?" He answered the question by stating that black people will not be satisfied until police brutality, segregation, and poverty cease.

Finally, King described his dream for America's future as a dream where people of all races would be able to work together, pray together, and stand up for freedom together in a nation where his own children "will not be judged by the color of their skin, but by the content of their character." King's moving speech and the March on Washington showed the Kennedy administration that civil rights was a pressing issue, paving the way for the Civil Rights Act of 1964.

This student does a nice job of weaving the most significant quotes of King's speech into her own interpretation. In the process, she delivers the three major themes of the oration, along with some keen insight. First, she recognizes King's juxtaposition of civil rights with the abolition of slavery one hundred years earlier. For King, Lincoln may have freed the slaves, but the children and grandchildren of those slaves were still the victims of the enduring legacy of slavery—racial discrimination. Second, she distinguishes King's plea for an integrated and nonviolent approach to change from the "new militancy" that was emerging among younger black nationalists at the time. This is a critical distinction to make because of the eventual shift in the civil rights movement to the militancy of Malcolm X and segregated emphasis of groups like the Black Panthers.[9] Third, the student offers a very valuable insight in her interpretation of the Kennedy administration and its reluctance to act more forcefully on the issue of civil rights. King was, in fact, addressing the president when he alluded to those who were asking him "When will you be satisfied?" King responds with a call to end all of the injustices suffered by his people; the very same injustices that were addressed in the Civil Rights Act of 1964.[10] Thus, the student's final statement that the speech forced the administration to act on the civil rights issue and "paved the way for the Civil Rights Act of 1964" are given strong support.

Analyzing Broadsides and Letters

Speeches, declarations, and pamphlets are not the only primary source documents I use with students. They are simply an introduction to more difficult and unique documents that individual students will have to engage for their particular local history research project during the winter months. By practicing their critical thinking skills with these better-known documents, students should feel more confident when reviewing others that are unique to their topic. Two very different primary source documents used by students in their local history research papers follow. The first is a broadside issued by General George Washington, Commander of the Continental Army, during the Valley Forge winter encampment of 1777–78.[11] The student, whose analysis follows, was writing his research paper on the significance of the Valley Forge encampment to the Revolutionary War.

DOCUMENT 4:

By His EXCELLENCY

GEORGE WASHINGTON, Esquire,

GENERAL and COMMANDER in CHIEF of the Forces

of the United States of America

BY Virtue of the Power and Direction to Me especially given,

I hereby enjoin and require all Persons residing within seventy Miles of my Head Quarters to thresh one Half of their Grain by the 1st Day of February, and the other Half by the 1st Day of March next ensuing, on Pain, in Case of Failure of having all that shall remain in Sheaves after the Period above mentioned, seized by the Commissaries and Quarter-Masters of the Army, and paid for as Straw

GIVEN *under my Hand, at Head Quarters, near the Valley Forge, in Philadelphia County, this 20th Day of December, 1777.*

G. WASHINGTON.

By His Excellency's Command,

ROBERT H. HARRISON, Sec'y.

LANCASTER: PRINTED BY JOHN DUNLAP

STUDENT ANALYSIS:

This order was given by General George Washington of the Continental Army to the farmers who lived within 70 miles the Valley Forge encampment. The order is dated December 20, 1777. The farmers are being ordered to "thresh one Half of their Grain by the 1st Day of February and the other Half by the 1st Day of March." If they refuse to do this, the grain will be "seized by the Commissaries and Quarter-Masters of the Army, and paid for as Straw," which would, of course, bring a lower price.

Washington gave this order because Congress did not provide the army with sufficient food or clothing. By December, the army was in a desperate condition. But Washington also probably realized that he was in a vulnerable situation with these farmers. He needed their grain to feed his army and their support to win the war. That is why he intended to pay the farmers for their grain. This document shows the desperate circumstances of the Continental Army in the winter of 1777.

The student had already completed some general background reading on the Valley Forge encampment, which is indicated by the contextual statements in his analysis. He used this document in his final paper as evidence of

Washington's dire straits and Congress' refusal to provide the necessary provisioning and financial support to ensure victory over the British army. His thesis was that Valley Forge was a major turning point in the War for American Independence because the army was not only able to survive the harsh winter months, but also became transformed into a disciplined fighting force through rigorous training there. That training and a military alliance with France enabled the American army to defeat the British.

This same argument has been made by several historians, and, to be sure, the student read some of that historiography.[12] However, he also had to collect and engage a specific body of primary source evidence to prove the argument on his own terms. In the process, his analysis of this broadside, among other documents, allowed him to have a first-hand experience with the craft of history and prove the argument in his own creative way.

The next document is a letter dated 1860 from Thomas Garrett, a Wilmington, Delaware, Quaker, to William Still, a free black member of the Pennsylvania Anti-Slavery Society. Both of these men were stationmasters on the Underground Railroad, a clandestine route to freedom in the North for slaves escaping bondage in the South.

DOCUMENT 5:
Wilmington, 12th Mo. 1st, 1860

RESPECTED FRIEND, WILLIAM STILL: I write to let thee know that Harriet Tubman is again in these parts. She arrived last evening from one of the trips of mercy to God's poor, bringing two men with her as far as New Castle. I agreed to pay a man last evening to pilot them on their way to Chester County [Pennsylvania]. The wife of one of the men, with two or three children, was left some thirty miles below, and I gave Harriet ten dollars to hire a man with a carriage to take them to Chester County. She said a man had offered for that sum, to bring them on. I shall be very uneasy about them, until I hear they are safe. There is now much more risk on the road, till they arrive here, than there has been for several months past, as we find that some poor worthless wretches are constantly on the look out on two roads, that they cannot well avoid, especially with carriage; yet as it is Harriet, who seemed to have had a special agent to guard her on her journey of mercy, I have hope.

Thy friend,
Thomas Garrett[13]

STUDENT ANALYSIS:

Thomas Garrett is a white Quaker station master from Wilmington, Delaware. He is writing to William Still in Philadelphia. Still is a free black member of the

Pennsylvania Anti-Slavery Society and the secretary of Philadelphia's General Vigilance Committee. His job was to communicate with all the station masters from Delaware to Canada so he could pass runaway slaves on to freedom. In this letter, written on December 1, 1860, Garrett informs Still that the famous black conductor Harriet Tubman is traveling through southeastern Pennsylvania guiding runaways to freedom on "her journey of mercy." He has given a man $10 to take them from Wilmington across the Mason-Dixon Line into Chester County. Although he worries that they will not be safe because of the "worthless wretches" or slave catchers who are "on the lookout" for them, Garrett believes that God will guide her. This letter is important because it shows that blacks and whites worked together in helping runaway slaves.

This student has also completed some general background reading on the Underground Railroad. She used this letter in her research paper as evidence of interracial support among stationmasters and conductors on the Underground Railroad. Because of the clandestine nature of this antebellum passage to freedom, she had to be very careful in analyzing such letters. For example, she had to understand, beforehand, that Harriet Tubman (often referred to by Garrett as the "Moses of her people") was conducting a "journey of mercy"— Garrett's reference for a journey North to freedom for runaway slaves. Similarly, "worthless wretches" was his synonym for "slave catchers." While the student also appears to acknowledge Garrett's belief that "God will protect" Tubman, she does not identify the Almighty as Tubman's "special agent," another one of Garrett's encoded terms. Professional historians have already identified the fact that Garrett and Still used code words to hide their true intent in their correspondence. Had they been caught harboring fugitives, they would have faced heavy fines and imprisonment as well as jeopardized the lives of the runaways. In fact, Garrett was so concerned about this danger that he destroyed all of Still's letters immediately after reading them.[14] Still, on the other hand, took a great risk by hiding all of Garrett's letters so that he could later publish them along with dozens of interviews of fugitives who came into his care. The resulting book, *The Underground Railroad,* published in 1872, continues to be the most accurate source on this clandestine route to freedom and a treasure trove of insight for historians of the antebellum period.

The other important point raised by this student is the reference to interracial cooperation. When she began the process of topic selection it was clear to me that she was fascinated by the covert aspects of the Underground Railroad. But I wanted her to go beyond that to find a more creative approach to the topic than the traditional historiography suggests. In the case of the Underground Railroad, white Quakers have too often been given credit for the success of the enterprise. Only in the last few years has the free black community been credited with a more aggressive role in the Underground Railroad than the historiography suggests.[15] This student, who argued that the success of Philadelphia's Underground Railroad depended on both the free black and white Quaker communities, did an effective job of using Garrett's letters to prove this point.

Analyzing Photographs

Besides letters, broadsides, speeches, and pamphlets, my students use a variety of other primary source documents in their research. Among the most fascinating are photographs, because students, especially visual learners, can relate with the human element revealed by them.

Photography was one of the most important inventions of the nineteenth century. For the first time it was possible to know the exact appearance of people, objects, and events that could not be viewed before. The first photograph appeared in 1839 and was called a daguerreotype, an image formed on a silver-coated copper plate. The daguerreotype appeared so life-like that it was called a "mirror with a memory." Whereas the painter could romanticize a person's features, the daguerreotype told the truth—for better or worse. Nevertheless, daguerreotypes became so popular that it seemed everyone wanted to be immortalized.

By the 1850s, the development of the glass plate negative allowed for multiple copies of a photograph to be made. The daguerreotype became obsolete and a new form, the carte de visit, appeared.[16] The Civil War generated an even greater demand for photographs, especially portraits of the common soldier. These images recorded for posterity a moment of great pride in the life of the subject. For especially young volunteers eager to fight, the photograph captured a rite of passage to manhood. Those who held rank were particularly proud and wanted to be photographed in full military regalia. Such was the case for sixteen-year-old Galusha Pennypacker of rural Pennsylvania (see Figure 1–1).

A restless youngster who yearned for greater adventure than farm life could provide, Pennypacker enlisted in the 9th Pennsylvania Volunteers when war broke out in 1861. He quickly distinguished himself as a responsible, charismatic soldier and was elected quartermaster. If you examine carefully the youngster's pose and expression, you can get an idea of the kind of impression he wanted to convey about his character. Smiling, for example, was not popular as it suggested frivolity or a lack of seriousness. Looking directly into the camera, on the other hand, suggested forthrightness and honesty. Gazing away from the lens suggested thoughtfulness in a man and modesty in a woman.

Figure 1–1. *Galusha Pennypacker*
(Courtesy of Chester County Historical Society)

Just as pose and expression revealed a person's character, their clothing often described their social status. Props were also used to convey a subject's wealth or accomplishments. Books, for example, indicated a good education or a scholarly bent. Additional rules applied for group portraits. The most important person dominated the photo by being placed at its focal point, with others surrounding that person a slight distance away as a sign of respect. The dominant person might also be seated, while others were standing. This is especially the case in family portraits where the male head of the house reminded the viewer of patriarchal authority. Gestures of affection were unusual because it was not acceptable to show such emotions in public.

Photographs and illustrations are among the most useful sources for studying history because they can recreate the atmosphere of a time period, indicate styles of clothing during a particular era, or reveal insight into an individual's personality. But to use photographs effectively as a research tool, a student must have some background knowledge of history to analyze them. The amount of evidence as well as the type of evidence that can be extracted from a photograph will depend on how much a student already knows about the topic. The more knowledge, the richer the photograph becomes as a source.

How do you read a photograph though? Much like a book: from left to right, then downward. Break down the photo into smaller components (i.e., background, foreground, groups of objects or people) and examine each one carefully. Review the photograph several times, trying to identify something you might have missed each time. Ask yourself some general questions about the action(s), people, buildings, or event being portrayed. In order to think through these issues, I provide my students with the following photograph chart (Figure 1–2) for each photo they intend to use in their research paper.

I am fairly lenient when grading photographic analyses. I am primarily concerned that students make an earnest effort to tell me as much as they can about the photograph and apply any previous knowledge about the subject matter. Those students who are good abstract thinkers will excel at this exercise.

Directions: Complete this chart and attach a photocopy of the photograph you have studied

NAME: _____

1. *First Reactions:* Jot down whatever first impressions you get about the photograph itself, the persons or objects in the photo, or your feelings.

2. *Detailed Examination:* List all the observable facts in the photo (i.e., people, objects, actions).

3. *Facts known from other sources:* Indicate here the actual place and date of the photo if not on the photo itself, the names of the people portrayed.

4. *Characteristic expression* or special relationships of persons or objects in the photo.

5. *Describe the mood of the photograph:* Formal, candid, happy, unhappy, indifferent.

6. *Considered reactions:* Jot down how you feel about the photograph now that you have studied it and answered any questions you may have had.

Figure 1–2. *Photograph Chart*

Figure 1–3. *Frederick Douglass (ca. 1848)*
(Courtesy of Chester County Historical Society)

They have a knack for translating the descriptive into some good, keen insight. For these students, a "picture" is indeed worth "a thousand words." Other students, who tend to be more concrete in their thinking, have more difficulty. The next two photographs (Figures 1–3 and 1–4) and student analyses reflect this point.

STUDENT PHOTOGRAPH ANALYSIS: FREDERICK DOUGLASS

1. *First reactions:* Jot down whatever first impressions you get about the photograph itself, the persons or objects in the photo, or your feelings.

   —old picture (daguerreotype)
   —young black man dressed in formal clothing
   —man is sad

2. *Detailed examination:* List all the observable facts in the photo (i.e., people, objects, actions).

—photo only shows face and chest
—dark clothing and white shirt
—bow tie around neck and some kind of rope

3. *Facts known from other sources:* Indicate here the actual place and date of the photo if not on the photo itself, the names of the people portrayed.

This is a rare photograph of a young Frederick Douglass, a former slave and the most well-known black abolitionist. Most photographs of Douglass were taken when he was older. This photograph was taken in 1848 when he was 30 years old.

4. *Characteristic expression* or special relationships of persons or objects in the photo.

Douglass appears to be reflecting on something in the distance. He has a slight smile on his face. He has strong features: a square jaw, high cheek bones and furrowed eye-brows. He looks determined. The light on his forehead reflects his light, mulatto features.

5. *Describe the mood of the photograph:* Formal, candid, happy, unhappy, indifferent.

The mood of the photograph is formal. Douglass is dressed formal. His hair is combed, not like the Afro he wears as an older man.

6. *Considered reactions:* Jot down how you feel about the photograph now that you have studied it and answered any questions you may have had.

I don't know whether Douglass is trying to pose as a refined person, or as an intellectual. The fact that he is formally dressed could indicate either one. He wants to be taken seriously, not like other black men who were considered intellectually and socially inferior at the time.

This particular student is a very good abstract thinker who was writing her research paper on nineteenth-century Philadelphia's anti-slavery movement and some of the more prominent black abolitionists who worked with the city's Quakers. Notice how she translates facial expressions with descriptive adjectives that may very well give us insight into Douglass' personality. The "furrowed eye-brows" and distant gaze suggest a "determined" posture. The student's considered reactions are even more impressive. Douglass' formal dress, the careful grooming of his hair as well as his expression all indicate to the student that the former slave wants to be "taken seriously."

In fact, Douglass had this daguerreotype taken in 1848 to give as a gift to Susan B. Anthony, a white Quaker reformer and champion of temperance,

Figure 1–4. *North Twentieth Street, bordering Shibe Park, during the 1929 World Series (Courtesy of Temple University Urban Archives, Philadelphia, PA)*

abolition, and women's rights. He had met Anthony in Rochester, New York, where her family lived. Douglass had settled in Rochester a year earlier to begin publishing an anti-slavery newspaper titled *The North Star*.

The image originally appeared in a small leather case, framed by a brass mat and was intended to be held in the hand by its viewer. It is also an intimate likeness rather than an enobling one, meant to be given to a close friend or loved one—not for public display. In this sense, the Douglass daguerreotype is a powerful illustration of a personal friendship that transcended the boundaries of race and gender; something that was extremely rare in antebellum society. The daguerreotype is also rare because it is one of the very few images of Douglass as a young man, as the student noted. Over the last decade the Douglass daguerreotype has captured the interest of Ken Burns and other producers of historical documentaries. Because of that interest the image has appeared on several Public Broadcasting Station programs on the Civil War, the Mexican-American War, and, more recently, a series on Abraham Lincoln.[17]

Here's another photo analysis that I found to be particularly insightful. The student was writing his local history research paper on Shibe Park, the home ballpark of the Philadelphia Athletics Baseball Club from 1909 to 1954. His thesis statement argued that "in a city that was witnessing increased economic, ethnic and religious polarization during the early twentieth century, Shibe Park functioned as a melting pot, bringing fans of diverse backgrounds together for the common purpose of cheering on their team." Among the photographs the student selected for his paper was the one shown in Figure 1–4, depicting fans lining the street bordering Shibe Park and others sitting atop the rowhouses which overlooked the right field fence.

STUDENT PHOTOGRAPHIC ANALYSIS:
PHILADELPHIA'S SHIBE PARK

Shibe Park never had trouble attracting fans. During the 1929 World Series, the ballpark was filled to capacity, but that did not prevent the city's immigrants and first-generation Americans from building roof-top bleachers on top of the row houses bordering the right field fence. From that vantage point, fans had a clear view of the playing field. This photograph, taken in October of 1929, shows that Shibe Park was an intimate part of the urban landscape of North Philadelphia. The street resembles the midway of a state fair with vendors selling food and souvenirs. Fans, some in suits and fedora hats, others in more modest clothing, can be seen sitting in the second-story windows and on the roof-tops of the row houses lining North Twentieth Street. Many of those fans worked in the factories that can be seen in the distant background. It is a scene of mass democracy where different social groups have come together through bleacher friendships, an intense team loyalty and hero-worship of almost mythological proportions.

I was impressed with this analysis for two reasons. First, students tend to shy away from photo analyses of landscapes. Generally speaking, landscapes are difficult for them to relate with, being devoid of human emotion. This student not only accepted the challenge, but in the process recreated the atmosphere of the North Philadelphia neighborhood surrounding Shibe Park at a particular point in history. Second, his analysis is remarkably creative as it places the people, dwellings, and factories of the photo in the larger context of his thesis, that is, "baseball as a vehicle for the assimilation into American society of immigrants and their children." If there is a shortcoming in this analysis, it deals with the relationship between the dress of the fans and their socioeconomic class. During the 1920s, most men, regardless of class, tended to dress in suits and hats when they went to the ballpark. While some of these "bleacher bums"

Figure 1–5. *"King Andrew the First," 1832*
(Courtesy of Library of Congress)

may very well have come from more affluent neighborhoods outside of North Philadelphia, thereby explaining their more affluent clothing, the World Series was a major social event for all classes and it would not be unusual to dress in formal clothing for the occasion.[18]

Analyzing Cartoons

Cartoons are perhaps the most enjoyable documents for high school students. The power of a good cartoon comes with the artist's ability to inform, entertain, and persuade the viewer. Cartoons are symbolic, subtle, and ironic depictions of a person or an event that can be used for a summary writing activity, such as a review test essay. Like photographs and documents, cartoons require background information in order for the student to understand their meaning. As students become more familiar with cartoons they can move from simply describing the action taking place to a clear explanation of the cartoon's message. Figure 1–5 is a cartoon of President Andrew Jackson, titled, "King Andrew The First" and one student's response in a review test essay on his presidency.

STUDENT CARTOON ANALYSIS: 'KING' ANDREW JACKSON

Andrew Jackson was a strong supporter of states rights and catered to the interests of the common man. This cartoon is inaccurate and was probably a piece of Republican propaganda, portraying Jackson as a king with little regard for the United States constitution. In fact, Jackson did not wield his veto power arbitrarily as suggested here, rather he used it to defend the interests of the common man and appealed to the masses for the support of his actions. His decisions with regard to the 1828 tariff, the Maysville Road bill and the Second Bank of the United States reinforce this point.

In 1828, before Jackson became president, the tariff of abominations was passed by Congress. This was an import tax on certain enumerated goods that affected many Americans. When he became president, Jackson signed a compromise treaty which called for a gradual reduction of this tax so it would not hurt the American farmer, in particular, who comprised 75% of the population.

In 1830, Jackson vetoed the Maysville Road bill in Kentucky because he did not believe that federal revenue should be used for an internal improvement that would only benefit one state. He believed that the Constitution did not support such a project because it would not benefit all or even most of the American people. He did, however, spend over $1 million a year on other internal improvements across the country. So while the cartoon shows Jackson's disregard for internal improvements and the U.S. Constitution, both of which he is stepping on, he was, in fact defending the latter by vetoing the former.

In 1832, Jackson vetoed an act to re-charter the Second Bank of the United States, again, because he believed that to do so was against the interests of the common man. Instead, he devised a plan to deposit all federal monies into state banks. He intended the states to use this money to support the needs of their own citizens. Jackson did this with the approval of the American people, who he appealed to for support. Also, Jackson had always been suspicious of the Second Bank. He knew that it was the beneficiary of wealthy elites who acted on their own interests rather than the common good. In this sense the caricature of Jackson has a good reason to step on the U.S. Bank, though it is mis-appropriately dressed in a king's robe.

When Jackson left office, he was praised as the "People's President" because he acted according to the needs and interests of the common man and within a democratic system. A king, as portrayed in this cartoon, does not usually have that kind of widespread popular support. Instead he wields his power arbitrarily and is answerable to few, if any. In short, the depiction of "King Andrew" is nothing more than a myth created by his political opponents.

Indeed, the cartoon of "King Andrew" was drafted by Jackson's political opponents, the Whig Party, which played on the president's uncompromising tactics. Despite Jackson's use of rhetoric that suggested ideological rigidity, he was a pragmatist whose positions shifted with events. The student's use of the Maysville Road veto is a good example. In 1830 he did veto the bill because it would have authorized the use of federal funds to build a road in Kentucky, a Whig stronghold. His veto made a states' rights case against federally financed internal improvements. At the same time, Jackson proved to be flexible. He later supported an annual average of $1.3 million in internal improvement bills that extended to every part of the country.[19]

Similarly, Jackson had long opposed the U.S. Bank because he believed that it was an example of a special privilege monopoly that hurt the common man. Not only was he determined to veto the bill, but also decided to carry his case to the public. His veto message condemning the bank as undemocratic, un-American, and unconstitutional stirred the emotions of voters, cleverly turning the issue into a struggle between the people and aristocracy. In so doing, Jackson not only oversimplified the issue, but made the bank into a symbol of everything that worried Americans in an era of change. In the Election of 1832, his political enemies, the Whigs, drafted and widely published the "King Andrew the First" cartoon to rally the common people against him. It didn't work. Jackson won handsomely, outpolling Henry Clay, the Whig candidate, and William Wirt, the Anti-Mason candidate, by 124,000 votes.[20]

While the student might have argued that the cartoon was an accurate reflection of Jackson's use of the veto and still received an "A" since she did so persuasively, her argument that Jackson used executive power in the name of the people and justified his actions by popular appeals to the electorate was well stated and convincingly proven.

Another cartoon, "The World's Constable," came to be a memorable image in American diplomacy as President Theodore Roosevelt sought to make the United States a policeman of the entire world. (See Figure 1–6.)

Figure 1–6. *The World's Constable*
(Cartoon by Louis Dalrymple, Judge, January 7, 1905, The Granger Collection)

STUDENT CARTOON ANALYSIS:
THE WORLD'S CONSTABLE

This cartoon illustrates President Theodore Roosevelt's "Big Stick" diplomacy, or as he said, "Walk softly and carry a big stick" in matters of diplomacy. As president from 1901 to 1909, Roosevelt pursued an activist policy in Latin America (as reflected by the Brazilian, Filippino and Columbian farmers to his right), Asia and the Middle East (as reflected by the figures directly under his "Big Stick"), and in Europe (as reflected by the figures to his left, who are like Britain, appealing for assistance, or like Russia, making accusations). Roosevelt believed in personal intervention rather than allowing the State Department to do his work. An example of this occurred in 1902 when Germany and Britain blocked Venezuelan ports until that country paid its defaulted debts. Worried that German influence would replace the British, he insisted that these European countries accept arbitration of the disputed financial claims and threatened to move U.S. battleships to Venezuela to enforce his intentions. The parchment TR holds under his left arm reflects the former, or passive diplomatic strategy, while the "Big Stick" in his right hand reflects the latter, or more aggressive diplomatic strategy.

Two years later, in 1904, when the Dominican Republic was bankrupt and plagued by a civil war, European creditors threatened to take advantage of that struggle collecting their debts. The threat forced TR to issue his corollary to the Monroe Doctrine, which stated that the United States would exercise international police power in the Western Hemisphere and any European country who wanted to collect debts should deal with him in Washington. Thus, the figure of TR in a policeman's uniform bridging the gap between Europe and Central America.

This student offers a solid explanation of the Roosevelt corollary to the Monroe Doctrine and the president's activist foreign policy. He also ties his explanation convincingly to a description of the cartoon. What is missing, however, is the historical context. Why, for example, did Roosevelt believe that he had to pursue such an activist policy? Why are some of the characters in the cartoon expressing anger and others appealing for help?

To be sure, Theodore Roosevelt inspired some countries and inflamed others. While he willingly shouldered the responsibilities of world power in the affairs of Latin America, he angered Germany, Britain, and Russia—who had claims in Central America—with his corollary to the Monroe Doctrine. Nor did he win favor with Columbia in supporting a Panamanian revolt in order to gain U.S. control over the canal zone. At home, he broke precedents in foreign policy by acting independently of Congress (shown by the smaller-sized capitol building underneath him) and often threatened to invoke force in defense of a broadly defined national security, if necessary.

Roosevelt assumed this "Big Stick" diplomacy at a critical time in United States history. The nation was in the midst of an industrial revolution and hoped to create foreign markets for its products. Consistent with this objective was Roosevelt's emphasis on a powerful navy. He realized that control of the seas meant control of foreign ports and, thus, more economic prosperity for the United States. The building and control of a canal in Panama was essential to these goals, as was Roosevelt's commanding presence on the world stage.[21]

Summary

Regardless of the medium, speeches, letters, photographs, and cartoons are the "stuff of history." Although they present a particular bias given at a particular period of time, documents also bring students face to face with the actual words and images of the people who shaped the past. In the process, documents can help students understand the human element of history, personalizing it in a way that no textbook can. In Part Two, we will explore the ways in which documents can be integrated into "present history" or students' written interpretations of the past.

Endnotes

1. Most of the documents are given to students in excerpt form, no more than two or three pages in length. The documents, in chronological order, are: John Winthrop, "A Model of Christian Charity," 1630; Thomas Paine, "Common Sense," 1776 ; Abigail Adams, "Selected Letters to John Adams," 1762–1776; Thomas Jefferson, "Declaration of Independence," 1776; Framers, "United States Constitution," 1789, 1791; James Madison, "Federalist No. 10," 1787; George Washington, "Farewell Address," 1797; Thomas Jefferson, "First Inaugural Address," 1801; Alexis de Tocqueville, "Democracy in America," 1835, 1840; "Native American Testimony to Trail of Tears," 1837, 1838; Catharine Beecher, "Treatise on Domestic Economy," 1841; Lucretia Mott and Elizabeth Cady Stanton, "Declaration of Sentiments," 1848; Harriet Beecher Stowe, "Uncle Tom's Cabin," 1852; Henry D. Thoreau, "Walden," 1854; Abraham Lincoln, "First Inaugural Address," 1861; Lincoln, "Gettysburg Address," 1863; Chief Joseph, "Surrender Speech," 1877; Andrew Carnegie, "Gospel of Wealth," 1889; Frederick Jackson Turner, "Frontier Thesis," 1893; Booker T. Washington, "Up From Slavery" 1901; Woodrow Wilson, "Fourteen Point Plan," 1919; "Selected Letters to President Roosevelt from Americans during the Great Depression," 1932–1941; Franklin D. Roosevelt, "Four Freedoms Speech," 1941; Harry S. Truman, "Truman Doctrine," 1946; "Brown v. Board of Education," 1954; John F. Kennedy, "Inaugural Address," 1961; Martin Luther King, Jr., "I Have A Dream Speech," 1963; Lyndon B. Johnson, "Great Society Speech," 1964; National Organization of Women, "Statement of Purpose," 1966; *New York Times,* "Pentagon Papers," 1971; Senate Judiciary Committee, "Watergate Hearings," 1973; and Justice Harry A. Blackmun, "Roe v. Wade Abortion Decision," 1973.

Documents can be found in the following editions: Henry S. Commager, editor. *The Blue and The Gray.* (New York: Fairfax Press, 1982); Henry S. Commager and Richard B. Morris, editors. *The Spirit of 'Seventy-Six: The Story of the American Revolution As Told By Participants.* (New York: Bonanza, 1983); Jack P. Greene, editor. *Settlements to Society, 1607–1763: A Documentary History of Colonial America.* (New York: Norton, 1975); and *Colonies to Nation, 1763–1789: A Documentary History of the American Revolution.* (New York: Norton, 1975); Richard D. Heffner, editor. A Documentary History of the United States. (New York: Mentor, 1991); Robert S. McElvaine, editor. *Down & Out in the Great Depression: Letters from the Forgotten Man.* (Chapel Hill: University of North Carolina, 1983); Peter Nabakov, editor. *Native American Testimony: An Anthology of Indian and White Relations* (1978); and National Archives and Records Administration, *Teaching With Documents.* (Washington D.C.: National Archives and Records Administration & National Council for Social Studies, 1989).

2. Thomas Paine, "Common Sense," (1776) in *Colonies to Nation, 1763 to 1789*, 275–82.

3. For those historians who credit Paine's *Common Sense* as the mobilizing force for Revolution, see: Bernard Bailyn, *Faces of Revolution. Personalities and Themes in the Struggle for American Independence*. (New York: Alfred A, Knopf, 1990), 67–68, 84); Philip Davidson, *Propaganda and the American Revolution, 1763–1783*. (New York: Norton, 1973), 215; Eric Foner, *Tom Paine and Revolutionary America*. (New York: Oxford University, 1976), 79–82; and Isaac Kramnick, "Editor's Introduction" to *Common Sense* by Thomas Paine. (New York: Penguin, 1982), 29.

4. Nearly 120,000 copies of *Common Sense* were sold in the first three months after its January 10, 1776, release. By the end of the year, about 500,000 copies had found their way into bookstores, private libraries, and taverns in both Europe and America. [See Moncure Daniel Conway, editor, *Writings of Thomas Paine*. (4 vols., New York, 1894–98), I: 67–69].

5. See John Keane, *Tom Paine: A Political Life*. (Boston: Little, Brown & Co., 1995), 135–38.

6. See "The Seneca Falls Declaration and Resolutions on Woman's Rights," in Thomas A. Bailey and David M. Kennedy, editors. *The American Spirit: United States History As Seen By Contemporaries* (2 vols. Lexington, MA: D.C. Heath & Co., 1984, 5th edition), Vol. I, pp. 327–31.

7. See Margaret Hope Bacon, *Valiant Friend: The Life of Lucretia Mott*. (New York: Walker & Company, 1980), 124–38; and Bacon, *Mothers of Feminism: The Story of Quaker Women in America*. (New York: Harper and Row, 1986), 101–19.

8. Martin Luther King, Jr., "The March on Washington Address," (1963) in *Great American Speeches*, edited by Gregory R. Suriano. (New York: Gramercy Books, 1993), 239–43.

9. For more information about the evolution of the civil rights movement from the nonviolent approach of Martin Luther King, Jr., to the militancy of Malcolm X, see: Stephen B. Oates, *Let the Trumpet Sound. The Life of Martin Luther King, Jr*. (New York: Harper & Row, 1982), 437–62; and Harris Wofford, *Of Kennedys & Kings: Making Sense of the Sixties*. (Pittsburgh: University of Pittsburgh Press, 1980), 178–239.

10. For more information on the impact of the March on Washington on the Kennedy Administration, see: Arthur M. Schlesinger, Jr., *A Thousand Days. John F. Kennedy in the White House*. (Boston: Houghton Mifflin Company, 1965), 950–77; and Taylor Branch, *Parting the Waters: America in the King Years, 1954–1963*. (New York: Simon & Schuster, 1989), 883–87. It is important to note that President Lyndon B. Johnson actually pushed the Civil Rights Bill of 1964 through Congress, but the Kennedy Administration was the architect of that bill and Johnson evoked the memory of the martyred president as a means of persuasion—among others—for Congress to pass it. [See Doris Kearns, *Lyndon Johnson and the American Dream*. (New York: Harper & Row, 1976), 190–92].

11. George Washington, "General Orders," December 20, 1777, in *The Writings of George Washington*, edited by John C. Fitzpatrick. (39 vols., Washington, D.C., 1931–1944), X: 150–51.

12. For the historiography on Valley Forge, see: E. Wayne Carp, *To Starve the Army at Pleasure. Continental Army Administration and American Political Culture, 1775–1783.* (Chapel Hill: University of North Carolina Press, 1984), 33–53; John W. Jackson, *Valley Forge: Pinnacle of Courage.* (Gettysburg, PA: Thomas Publications, 1992); John F. Reed, *Valley Forge, Crucible of Victory.* (Monmouth Beach, NJ, 1969); Charles Royster, *A Revolutionary People at War. The Continental Army and American Character, 1775–1783.* (New York: W.W. Norton, 1979); John B. B. Trussell, Jr., *Birthplace of an Army: A Study of the Valley Forge Encampment.* (Harrisburg, PA: Pennsylvania Historical and Museum Commission, 1979).

13. Thomas Garrett to William Still, December 12, 1860, quoted in William Still, *The Underground Railroad* (1872) (reprinted by Johnson Publishing Company of Chicago, 1970), 530–31.

14. See James A. McGowan, *Station Master on the Underground Railroad: The Life and Letters of Thomas Garrett.* (Moylan, PA: Whimsie Press, 1977), 85–90.

15. See Charles L. Blockson, "The Underground Railroad: The Quaker Connection," in *For Emancipation and Education: Some Black and Quaker Efforts, 1680–1900*, edited by Eliza Cope Harrison. (Philadelphia: Awbury Arboretum Association and Germantown Historical Society, 1997), 39–43; James O. Horton and Lois E. Horton, *In Hope of Liberty: Culture, Community and Protest Among Northern Free Blacks, 1700–1860.* (New York: Oxford University Press, 1997); and Jane Rhodes, *Mary Ann Shadd Cary. The Black Press and Protest in the Nineteenth Century.* (Bloomington, IN: Indiana University Press, 1998).

16. See Floyd Rinhart and Marion Rinhart, *The American Daguerreotype.* (Athens: University of Georgia, 1981); William Welling, *Photography in America: The Formative Years, 1839–1900.* (Albuquerque: University of New Mexico, 1978); and Beaumont Newhall, *The Daguerreotype in America.* (New York: Dover Publications, 1976).

17. Pam Powell, "The Daguerreotype: Portraiture at the Dawn of Photography." Chester County Historical Society Exhibition: May 7 through November 24, 2001.

18. See William C. Kashatus, *Connie Mack's '29 Triumph. The Rise and Fall of the Philadelphia Athletics Dynasty.* (Jefferson, NC: McFarland & Company, 1999).

19. See Robert V. Remini, *Andrew Jackson and the Course of American Freedom, 1767–1845.* (3 vols., New York: Harper & Row, 1980–1984), II: 251–56.

20. *Ibid.*, 379–92.

21. See Edmund Morris, *Theodore Rex.* (New York: Random House, 2001), 183–92; H. W. Brands, *TR: The Last Romantic.* (New York: Basic Books, 1997), 463–88, 524–40, 567–92; and John Morton Blum, *The Republican Roosevelt.* (New York: Atheneum, 1974), 125–41.

Part Two: Present History
Position and Local History Research Papers

Analyzing documents and mastering factual content are critical to the writing process. But a student's understanding of historical subject matter lies in her or his ability to explain cause-and-effect relationships, interpret the significance of past events, and clearly articulate a position and defend it. These skills are best demonstrated through the writing of the position and research papers. I call these papers "present history" because they are contemporary interpretations of past events. They are also present history in the sense that today's students are, increasingly, integrating more progressive methods of analysis in their papers. Much like professional historians, students are being encouraged to explore the disciplines of psychology, anthropology, sociology, and statistics as a way to gain important insights into the past.[1] The social sciences also fascinate high school students whose earlier experience with history class tended to emphasize a dry, vocabulary textbook-controlled approach.

The position paper is a short composition that interprets a single subject and gives the view of the writer. Position papers can be given as a homework assignment or as a timed, in-class test. The advantage of the former is that students can process, over a longer period of time, their understanding of a subject and are permitted to consult the text. The timed, in-class test, on the other hand, is often used by teachers as a quick way to determine a student's mastery of the subject matter. I have used the position paper in both ways, though my expectations are, of course, higher for the take-home paper because students have a longer time period to produce the essay as well as to integrate factual material from the text.

Students will write an average of 8 to 10 position papers a year in my class. About half of those papers are in-class test essays, the other half are take-home assignments. More recently I have required that they save all of the graded papers in a portfolio that is handed in three or four times over the course of the school year. Portfolios allow me to see the "starting point" for each student as a writer, and to gain a better understanding of students' strengths and shortcomings, how to challenge them to become better writers, and to determine their growth as writers as the year progresses. I will discuss portfolios in greater depth in the conclusion.

There are three major steps in writing a quality position paper, whether it be an in-class test paper or a take-home assignment: (1) forming the argument; (2) writing; and (3) revising.[2]

Forming the Argument

Forming the argument is done by analyzing the question being asked. Students must learn to look at the words carefully. Often questions begin with one of three phrases: "compare and contrast"; "evaluate the following statement"; or "identify cause and effect." Students must be sure of what the question asks. Once that is done, the appropriate information should be collected and organized according to the themes that are to be developed in the argument. The best way to do this is to create a rough outline.

The outline begins with a thesis statement. This is the writer's position, or viewpoint, which should be delivered in no more than two sentences in the opening paragraph of the position paper. While the thesis reflects the student's personal position, it is *not* an opinion. By definition, an "opinion" does not require any substantive evidence; it is nothing more than the unsubstantiated feelings of the person holding it. A thesis, on the other hand, must be defended with factual support, concept, and a rational explanation. Accordingly, I do not allow my students to use the first person "I" in their writing of the position paper, such as "I believe . . ." or "I think . . ." The thesis, like the position paper itself, is to be written in the third person, narrative form. By doing so, the writer affords the necessary distance between her- or himself and unsubstantiated opinion, giving the paper a more forceful tone. The thesis statement also provides an organization for the essay by identifying those points to be addressed and in the same order they will appear in the paper. Often the thesis evolves from the information that has been gathered. But students must still take the time to think through their beliefs on the topic and how they will prove it with the information gathered. Let's take an example.

The following outline was completed by a student writing a take-home position paper on the question: "Compare and contrast President Franklin D. Roosevelt's New Deal policies with his management of the economy during

World War II. Which was more effective in bringing the country out of the Great Depression?"

I. Thesis: Although the New Deal was responsible for a degree of relief and recovery, America's war effort was much more effective in bringing the country out of the Depression. World War II immediately and drastically lowered the unemployment rate, raised farm income, and increased industrial productivity.

II. Body sections

    A: Unemployment rate

        1. New Deal:

            a. In 1933 nearly 25% unemployment.

            b. National Industrial Recovery Act—over $3 billion for public works

            c. By 1937, unemployment reduced to 15%

        2. World War II

            a. In 1942 unemployment reduced to 5%

            b. War industry demanded longer hours

            c. By 1944 unemployment lower than 2%

    B: Farm income

        1. New Deal

            a. 1933 farm foreclosures at all-time peak with more than 50,000.

            b. Agricultural Adjustment Act—paid farmers to cut production

        2. World War II

            a. Increased demand for food for soldiers and allies

            b. Higher prices, increased production added $20 billion to land value

            c. By 1945 farm foreclosures down to less than 5,000

    C: Industrial productivity

        1. New Deal

            a. 1933—83% drop in industrial production

            b. NRA created but little gains in industrial production

        2. World War II

            a. 1939—creation of Industrial Mobilization Plan

            b. 1945—U.S. industrial production doubled that of all Axis countries

III. Conclusion

This student had been experiencing some difficulties in organizing earlier position papers, so I asked him to turn in an outline to me before he wrote the paper. While students should be doing this on their own, I usually don't require them to hand in the outline for a take-home essay. When I do, they usually make a stronger effort to think through the argument before handing in the outline. As you can see, the outlining process gave this student a clearer understanding of the assignment by forcing him to examine, in a comparative way, the New Deal and World War II. Accordingly, the three measures of evaluation he chose—unemployment rate, farm productivity, and industrial production— flow out of his thesis statement and form the basis of the comparison. Note that he has also chosen to use statistical data to defend the thesis as each body section contains statistical information on both the New Deal and World War II. The outline reflects the comparative nature of the essay as well as the factual data necessary to prove the thesis. Now he is ready for the second stage of writing the position paper.

Writing the Position Paper

The writing stage begins with the formation of the introductory paragraph. The introduction should give the reader a clear idea of the topic being discussed and the author's viewpoint. A broad, general comment on the topic itself serves as a starting point. This opening statement serves to catch the reader's attention and to set the historical context of the essay by identifying the time period being discussed. Then the introduction gradually narrows the focus of the topic to the thesis statement itself, which is essentially an answer to the question being asked.

After completing the introductory paragraph, the student is ready to turn his attention to the body sections. In a position paper, the body sections may be only a paragraph in length, or they can be multiple paragraph sections. Here the factual information gathered to support the argument is presented in a way that demonstrates the student's understanding of the topic. I instruct students to offer at least two pieces of factual evidence to defend their thesis in each body section. One piece of evidence is too few and might be considered by the reader to be an "exception" rather than a "consistent pattern." Three pieces of evidence are too many for a position paper because of time constraints in an in-class test, or staying within a word count for a take-home essay. I don't care what type of evidence the students use. Primary source quotations, statistical data, and indisputable dates and events are all acceptable forms of evidence. More important is how that factual evidence is integrated into the argument.

Critical to good position paper writing is an effective integration of fact, concept, and explanation. Depending on how the facts have been organized in the outlining process, the student should, through inductive reasoning, be able to arrive at a main idea, or concept, for each group of facts. This main idea, or concept, is called a "topic sentence." Topic sentences should introduce each body section of the essay and should be crafted in a way that clarifies part of the thesis statement. The challenge, in the writing of the body sections, is to integrate the factual information with concept through an insightful explanation. Students must choose their words carefully, considering both the reasoning of the argument and the nouns, verbs, adjectives, and adverbs used.

The next step in the writing process is crafting a conclusion that holds the essay together by summarizing the main points already argued and providing the reader with an additional insight on the subject as it applies to the broader context of history or current events. I encourage students to read over the introduction and the body of the essay beforehand. In this way, they can write a conclusion that reinforces the thesis without simply repeating the introduction.

The final step is to arrive at a title that will tell the reader, at a glance, the subject matter of the essay. Too often, students use the question, or some form of it, as the title. Questions are *not* titles. Titles are statements that should answer the question being investigated. I encourage my students to use a "double title," or a general title that addresses the topic and a secondary title that reveals their position. These two titles are separated by a colon and should be "catchy" in order to capture the reader's interest. Here are some examples:

"A Virtuous Education: William Penn's Vision for Philadelphia's Schools"

"United States Foreign Policy: From Isolation to Global Policemen, 1935–49"

"America's Founding Fathers: Opportunists and Victims"

"Communism: Another Name for Clinical Paranoia"

"Molly Maguires: Anthracite Victims of Pennsylvania's Industrial Revolution"

Revising the Position Paper

The third and final stage of the writing process is revising the essay. After completing the initial draft, the student should read it over to check the spelling, style, punctuation, and consistency. Of primary importance is that the introduction and conclusion agree. Often, those students who have not analyzed the question very well will find that these two parts of the paper contradict each other. Students should also check for smooth transitions between body sections and between paragraphs. Other points to check include:

> Never use "slang" expressions if not contained in a primary source quote.
>
> Avoid contractions (i.e., use "did not" instead of "didn't")
>
> Do not assume that the reader is familiar with the topic. Explain yourself clearly.
>
> Avoid writing about process (i.e., "In this paper I am going to do the following...")
>
> Do not use terms such as "obviously" or "clearly" as it patronizes the reader.
>
> Avoid beginning a sentence with "It"; use a descriptive noun instead.

Assessment

If we return to the comparative essay on the New Deal and World War II, we now have a barometer against which we can measure the student's success in navigating the writing process.

"WORLD WAR II: THE ELIXIR TO THE GREAT DEPRESSION"

In October 1929 the stock market crashed and the Great Depression followed. To combat the devastating effects of the Depression, President Franklin D. Roosevelt proposed a series of legislative measures aimed at relief, recovery, and reform. Although this "New Deal" was responsible for a degree of relief and recovery, America's war effort was much more effective in bringing the country out of the Depression. World War II immediately and drastically lowered the unemployment rate, raised farm income, and increased industrial productivity.

America's wartime economy called for a larger, more efficient workforce than that which existed during the so-called "boom time," five years before the stock market crashed. At the depth of the Depression in 1933, nearly 25 percent of America's civilian labor force was unemployed. Roosevelt's New Deal offered some relief to the unemployed and, by 1937, the percentage was down to about 15 percent. Through the National Industrial Recovery Act, passed by Congress in 1933, a large scale public works spending program which employed millions was put into operation. More than $3 billion was turned over for public work projects in the hope that such government spending would prime America's pump. Over the next four years, government spending did stimulate the economy, yet over 7 million were still unemployed in 1937, and over 4 million families were on relief.

In 1942, however, just after the United States entered World War II, unemployment dropped to 5 percent. The nation actually found itself hard-pressed for sufficient numbers of people to serve in the armed forces, to man war plants, to farm and to keep the economy functioning. Not only did the previously unemployed find work, but women, children, and the elderly found work. With more than one family member working and with the legislatively mandated payment of time-and-a-half for overtime beyond 40 hours a week, the living standard of working people drastically improved. By 1944, the unemployment rate was under 2 percent.

World War II also gave a bigger boost to farm production than FDR's New Deal programs. During the Depression prices for agricultural goods were so low that the farmer could not survive without government aid. Farm defaults and foreclosures were at an all-time peak in 1933 when the Agricultural Adjustment Act was formed under the New Deal. Under this plan, the producers of basic commodities received payments for cutting production. This would cause the consumer to pay a higher price. The income of farmers did increase, but slowly, and farm income did not exceed the inadequate 1929 amount until 1941.

World War II caused a stockpiling mentality, both in America and in Europe. The United States felt the increased demand for food because of the need to feed the armed forces and provide relief to war-torn Europe. Six months after Pearl Harbor food shortages actually emerged. Higher prices and increased productivity allowed the farmers to increase the value of their land by $20 billion and save a total of $11 billion. Whereas the number of farm foreclosures broke 50,000 in 1933, by 1945, the number was less than 5,000.

The boost in industry provided by the New Deal also paled in comparison to the veritable boom in industrial production stimulated by large government military contracts during the war. During the Depression such industries as iron and steel manufacturing witnessed an 83 percent drop in production. The war reversed that trend. Even before Pearl Harbor, the Industrial Mobilization Plan of 1939 allowed for a significant increase in U.S. industrial production. Coal, steel, and other industries were open 24 hours a day, seven days a week to produce the fuel and materials for tanks, airplanes and naval vessels needed to win the war. By 1945, U.S. production was double that of all the Axis countries combined.

World War II was responsible for the rebirth of the American economy. The results were instant and dramatic. Whereas FDR's New Deal seemed merely to point the ailing economy in the right direction, the war provided the necessary economic stimulus for a decrease in the unemployment rate and increased growth in farm and industrial productivity.

The success of this position paper lies with its organization, statistical evidence, and insight. The reader, at a glance, can see how the various body sections grow out of the thesis statement. Each body section begins with a clear topic sentence that compares the overall effect of both the New Deal and World War II on a particular area of the U.S. economy. Each body section follows a predictable order. The New Deal's effect on the economy is addressed first followed by the war's effect. In most cases, the student offers two distinct pieces of statistical evidence to defend his argument. Although statistics can be manipulated to prove any thesis, he has carefully integrated the data into his argument and the rhetorical vocabulary he uses to prove his thesis. Consider the following statements he uses when discussing the effect of the New Deal on the economy:

> "Over the next four years, government spending did stimulate the economy, yet over 7 million were still unemployed in 1937, and over 4 million families were on relief."
>
> "Under the [Agricultural Adjustment Act], the producers of basic commodities received payments for cutting production. This would cause the consumer to pay a higher price. The income of farmers did increase, but slowly, and farm income did not exceed the inadequate 1929 amount until 1941."
>
> "The boost in industry provided by the New Deal also paled in comparison to the veritable boom in industrial production stimulated by large government military contracts during the war."

Note the descriptive vocabulary. Words such as "inadequate," "paled," and "cutting production" are used to describe the effect of the New Deal on the economy. On the other hand, he uses such terms as "larger," "more efficient," "drastically improved," "rebirth," "instant," and "dramatic" to distinguish World War II's more positive effect on the economy. These statements and the descriptive vocabulary they reveal can be considered the "rhetoric" of the position paper. They tie together the factual evidence with the concept in a persuasive explanation of the student's position. This is a learned skill that takes time to develop. This particular student was not able to offer the kinds of evidence or insightful explanation he has here at the beginning of the course. But as he continued to develop as a writer, he learned more subtle ways to defend his argument. Like a lawyer, he learned how to state his position, or what he intended to prove, clearly and concisely at the opening of the paper. He proceeds to offer the evidence to support his position as he develops his case through the body sections, and in language that will persuade his reader. Finally, he concludes by restating his position in more powerful language than that with which he opened the essay.

Nevertheless, this position paper received a B+ (88). What prevented the piece from being first-rate was that the student sometimes allowed the factual evidence to overwhelm his explanation. I would, for example, like to have seen him explore the economic theory of John Maynard Keynes and explain how FDR employed deficit spending during the Depression in the hope of restoring the economy. While the economy responded slowly, it never fully recovered until wartime expenditures, beginning in 1941, finally eliminated unemployment and ended the Depression.[3] This theory was emphasized both in the course and in the textbook.[4] In a take-home assignment such as this one, I expect a more comprehensive discussion of the material, especially when this particular essay begs the question: "Where did FDR get the money to increase employment, and farm and industrial production in the depths of a Depression?" The paper also falls short of answering the "So what?" question. That is, why is this topic important to us in the larger context of U.S. history and/or current events. I would have liked a further insight tacked onto the conclusion, for example, that would suggest that the kind of deficit spending FDR initiated during World War II became a standard economic policy in the post-War era and one that led to a crippling national deficit during and after the Nixon Administration.[5]

Diagramming the Position Paper

For other students, writing can be a frustrating experience, especially if they have a learning difference. I can empathize with them. I am a visually oriented learner who had difficulty as a student adapting to a more traditional linguistic approach. Fortunately, one of my high school teachers recognized that fact and taught me the mechanics of writing by diagramming the process. The mental image of the diagram allowed me to grow, significantly, as a writer, particularly during my college years when most history exams consisted of essay questions. The diagram is illustrated in Figure 2–1.

The inverted triangle represents the introduction, which students open with a general topic statement and gradually narrow the focus to the specific thesis they intend to argue in the paper. The graphic illusion of an inverted triangle gives students a visual reference of how to narrow the topic. The thesis statement is represented by a thin rectangle, consisting of three parts. These three parts are the specific themes that will be developed in the body of the position paper and give organization to the essay. Notice that each body section (indicated by a square) refers back to one part of the thesis. The top third of the square can be considered the topic sentence. Also notice that each square, or body section, has the numbers 1 and 2 inside of it. Those numbers remind students that they must offer two pieces of evidence to support their case in each body paragraph. Finally, the half moon at the bottom of the graphic represents the conclusion. Here students summarize the main points they have

Introduction

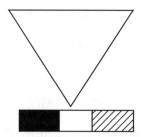

Thesis Statement

Body Section I

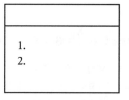

1.
2.

Body Section II

1.
2.

Body Section III

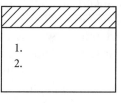

1.
2.

Conclusion

Figure 2–1. *Diagram of the position paper*

made in the paper and "round off" the essay with a further insight that applies the topic to the broader context of history or current events.

Let's examine the following position paper on the role of religion in colonial America and how it can be diagrammed. The question is: "Evaluate the following statement: 'Religion played an important role in shaping the social and political structure of Colonial America.'" This question was given as part of an in-class test at the beginning of the school year. In addition to the time element involved, there are other factors that necessarily limit the quality of this essay when compared to the previous one. The time element alone assures that the style and coherence of the essay will not be as polished as that in a take-home assignment. Since students are not permitted to refer to the text or to their notes during the 45-minute test period, there is also a limit on the caliber and quantity of evidence they can use to support their argument. Because this is also the first test of the school year, students are not familiar with the standards I have for writing, aside from a one-page handout I give them in order to prepare for an in-class test essay. That handout gives them a basic idea of how to organize the essay (already explained earlier in the book) and the above-mentioned diagram.

"RELIGION IN COLONIAL AMERICA"

Religion played one of the greatest roles in the lives of colonial Americans. Religion meant more to the colonists than simply a way to worship God. For some colonists, the reason for immigration to America was primarily based on the practice of their religion. For others, religion took a very political role. Whatever role religion did play, it helped to create the identity of the colonists in that regard.

In colonies such as Plymouth, Maryland, and Pennsylvania, the freedom to worship as they pleased was the reason for their establishment. In 1620, the Pilgrims established Plymouth Plantation as a place where they could freely practice the Puritan religion without being under the scrutiny of the Church of England. Similarly, Maryland was established by Lord Baltimore as a haven for practicing Catholics. William Penn established Pennsylvania in 1681 as a colony devoted to religious toleration. Penn was a Quaker who, like many of Pennsylvania's early settlers, had been persecuted by the British government for their non-conformist beliefs. Therefore, he opened his colony to a diverse group of religions drawn to the Quaker ideals of toleration, pacifism, and brotherly love.

Religion was the political and social foundation in Massachusetts and Rhode Island. When Massachusetts was established in 1629, the Puritans who founded it operated on a social hierarchy in which Visible Saints, or those pre-destined to salvation, were both the political and social leaders. The Governor, John Winthrop, and the General Court, which determined the laws, were Visible

Saints. There was no separation between Church and State. Next were the members of the church who could vote for representatives of the Court but could not serve on it. Finally, at the bottom of the ladder were the un-churched. Roger Williams established Rhode Island in 1636 because he opposed the Puritans belief in the unity of church and state. Williams settled in Providence with thirteen other non-conformists. There he established the first genuine democracy and church-divorced community in the colonies.

Religion played an important role in the establishment as well as the social and political foundations of colonial America during the 17th century. As the colonies moved toward the eighteenth century, Puritanism and Quakerism, to a degree, began to decline. But other religions, such as Presbyterianism and Methodism, began to rise and continued to play an important role in the lives of the colonists, paving the way for the many of the other freedoms we, as Americans, enjoy today.

If we were to diagram this position paper, the introduction would take the form of the inverted triangle. At the top of the triangle would be the reference to religion in the colonies, the general topic of the essay. The next sentence—"Religion meant more to the colonists than simply a way to worship God"—is a transition sentence that begins to narrow the focus of the essay. The thesis comes next: "For some colonists, the reason for immigration to America was primarily based on the practice of their religion. For others, religion took a very political role. Whatever role religion did play, it helped to create the identity of the colonists in that regard." Of course, the thesis statement is too long and it does not break down the argument as cleanly as it might have. But the thesis does give the reader a basic understanding of the organization and the argument to follow. The diagram of the introduction looks like this:

Religion played one of the greatest roles in the lives of colonial Americans.

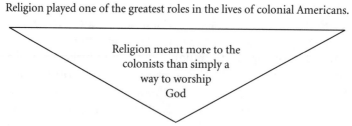

Religion meant more to the
colonists than simply a
way to worship
God

Thesis: For some colonists, the reason for immigration to America was
primarily based on the practice of their religion. For others, religion took a
very political role. Whatever role religion did play, it helped to create the
identity of the colonists in that regard.

The body sections of the paper come next. In this case there are only two body sections. The first discusses colonies that were established because of a desire for religious liberty, or the freedom to worship as one pleased. In this section, Plymouth, Maryland, and Pennsylvania are used as examples, or evidence. The second body section discusses religion as the social and political foundations of the colonies. Here Massachusetts and Rhode Island are used as examples. The diagram of these body sections look like this:

Body Section I

In some colonies, the freedom to worship was the reason for their establishment.
1. Plymouth 2. Maryland 3. Pennsylvania

Body Section II

Religion as political and social foundation in other colonies
1. Massachusetts 2. Rhode Island

The conclusion summarizes the essay with the statement: "Religion played an important role in the establishment as well as the social and political foundations of colonial America during the 17th century." The student provided a further insight in her observation that "as the colonies moved toward the eighteenth century, Puritanism and Quakerism, to a degree, began to decline. But other religions, such as Presbyterianism and Methodism, began to rise." She also gives the reader the historical significance of her topic with her final insight that the many religious groups that eventually settled in the colonies, "paved the way for many of the other freedoms we, as Americans, enjoy today." The diagram looks like this:

Religion played an important role in the establishment as well as the social and political foundations of colonial America during the 17th century. As the colonies moved toward the eighteenth century, Puritanism and Quakerism, to a degree, began to decline. But other religions, such as Presbyterianism and Methodism, began to rise and continued to play an important role in the lives of the colonists, paving the way for many of the other freedoms we, as Americans, enjoy today.

Local History Research Paper

The writing of a position paper is an excellent way to prepare for the term paper that has, sadly, become the only writing assignment in many American high school history classes. Position papers introduce the student to the organization, mechanics, and style of writing expected in the semester-long term paper. Unfortunately, most of the term papers written by high school students across this country are little more than a regurgitation of existing scholarship, or historiography. Some teachers even allow the text to be used as a major source for the paper. As a result, many high school students simply string together fragments of these established interpretations—or at least their understanding of them—slap their own name on the title page, and hand it in. They do not give their own interpretation of an event. They do not visit any special collections, or historical sites where the subject of their paper actually occurred. Few are based on a genuine engagement or understanding of primary source documentation. The topics are almost always national in scope and have been done thousands of times before. Many would not be written at all if the student had a choice in the matter, and few teachers would choose to read them if not paid to do so by their school district. Not surprisingly, in many American high schools, the term paper has become a painful process for both students and teachers because there is very little that is creative, intrinsically interesting, or personally relevant about the research and writing of them. Perhaps that is why so few teachers devote the time and attention that is required to develop good, solid writers.

I spent the first three years of my teaching career engaged in this fruitless exercise. After much frustration, I decided to abandon the traditional term paper for the more promising local history research paper. There were three good reasons for the decision. First, the local history research paper would restore a proper balance in the teaching of the discipline. I wanted my students to understand that American history involves a great deal more than the activities of prominent white men. The everyday experiences of ordinary men, women, and children in local towns and neighborhoods also gave shape to our nation's past. Local, family, and ethnic histories provide avenues into the lives of ordinary people, the places they lived, worked, and worshipped. Even professional historians, who once dismissed local history as "irrelevant," have, over the last few decades, recognized the extraordinary value of an increasing number of scholarly works that use individual communities as case studies in social history investigation.

Second, local history excites students. Because the local community is much like the family, it is less remote from the students' own interests and concerns, more concrete and easier to grasp. In both the family and the local community, students have a natural, vested interest because they live within it. The events, behaviors, and rules in both institutions shape the students' outlook, whether consciously or not. They also help to define the way students look at the larger world and, in many ways, themselves. For these reasons, local history has great potential to demonstrate to students that the study of the past can be vitally and intrinsically exciting as well as relevant to their own lives.

Third, local history provides students with a firsthand experience of the past. At the higher levels of education, the purpose of doing a research paper is to advance new evidence, or a new interpretation of a significant topic. But most high schools settle for a regurgitation of prominent events, emphasizing the library and writing skills needed to complete a term paper. "Doing history" involves much more. Students discover, perhaps for the very first time, the history and significance of a lesser-known figure, place, or event, and interpret it in the larger context of our nation's past. They come to understand that historical research involves more than a visit to the public or school library, but also visiting special collections, historical societies, and, in some cases, the historical site itself; some of which may never have been consulted by the scholars who wrote the accepted interpretations![6]

Finally, I was teaching in Philadelphia, a city that has limitless possibilities of subject matter. Founded in 1681 by the English Quaker William Penn, Philadelphia is one of the oldest cities in the nation and served as a convenient meeting place for members of the Continental Congresses, the Framers of the United States Constitution, and, for the decade of the 1790s, the nation's capital. Perhaps that is why many Philadelphians boast that "America starts here!" Because of the city's strong Quaker influence, the city also became a center of social reform during the nineteenth century. Some of the most significant humanitarian contributions were made in abolitionism, women's rights, temperance, health care, and prison reform. In all these ways, local history is synonymous with national history.

At the same time, Philadelphia has the history of a small town community, where less prominent events had a major impact on the social, political, and economic development of its neighborhoods. Its history includes the development of commuter suburbs, the assimilation of various ethnic groups, bossism's impact on local elections, and popular pastimes like the New Year's Day Mummer's Parade, the Dad Vail Regatta, and the Penn Relay Races. These events are more local in nature and, in many respects, are not very different from those that occurred in many other American cities, or even smaller towns. For all these reasons, I decided to introduce my students to the local history research paper.

Guidelines for the Research Paper

Each year my classes spent fourteen weeks on the research and writing process. Students were given the following guidelines:

1. Research papers must address one of Philadelphia's historic sites, a personality or group of people from the past, or a local event that had a regional, statewide, or national impact.

2. A research journal will be kept throughout the process. Students may be asked to submit the journal at any time during the 14-week process and must bring it to class on a daily basis. The journal will detail the following information each time you visit a library, special collection, or historic site, even if it is the same one:

   - name of the institution

   - date and time of visit

   - signature of the contact person (librarian, archivist, director)

   - useful information discovered (letters, newspapers, journals, maps, photographs)

   - your opinion on what resources were helpful and why

3. Research papers must address the significance of the person, group, place, or event in the broader framework of regional, state, and/or national history.

4. Research papers must be a minimum of six pages (approximately 1,500 words) in length, not including endnotes, bibliography, and appendices. The paper must be typed or word processed, double-spaced, and conform to the guidelines detailed in Turabian's *Manual for Writers.*[7]

5. Research papers must include the following sources: at least five bibliographic sources, not including general encyclopedias; at least three of the five sources must be primary sources; at least two photographs, contemporary or historic.

6. All work must be the student's own.

7. Each step of the following process must be approved before the student may go on to the next. Unsatisfactory work must be redone before a student is permitted to proceed. Failure to meet deadlines will result in a reduction of 5 points per school day for that particular step. Extensions, if absolutely necessary, must be requested and granted two days before the due date and must be accompanied with a note by a parent explaining the extenuating circumstances. The following deadlines will be enforced:

Topic Selection (5 points of final grade) Due at end of week 2

Preliminary annotated bibliography (10 points) Due at end of week 3

Photograph chart (10 points) Due at end of week 6

Introduction, thesis, and detailed outline with note-cards (15 points) Due end of week 8

First draft, including endnotes and final bibliography (30 points) Due at end of week 11

Peer evaluation (10 points) Due at end of week 12

Final draft (20 points) Due at end of week 14

8. A passing paper is required to receive credit for the course. A failing paper must be redone until it is passing.

9. Be sure to hand all work directly to the teacher. Do not place it in a mail box or on a desk. Save all steps until your final paper is returned.

These guidelines are designed to teach students accountability and to give them an appreciation for the fact that good writing is a process that takes place over a period of weeks, months, and, often, many years' time; they are not designed to stifle the creativity or put restraints on their exploration of a process. In fact, students are encouraged to continue their research up to the eleventh week of the process when their rough draft is due.

At the same time, it is extremely important for students to take each stage of the process seriously, putting forth their best effort. Each stage sets a foundation for the next. If students are not careful in the selection of a topic, for example, they might not find enough sources for the annotated bibliography. If the sources in the bibliography are not selected carefully, students will have difficulty finding the information to prove their hypothesis or thesis, which, of course, will be revealed in their outline. If the outline is not done carefully, then there will be problems developing the argument in the paper itself. Accountability is important, therefore, in each stage of the process it is cultivated by predetermined deadlines that allow the teacher checkpoints along the way and by the keeping of a research journal. The journals give me a better understanding of the trouble spots as well as the initiative the students are taking in the research process, they can be requested at any time during the process.

Where to Do Research

Since I have already established a contact person at each of the local research institutions, these partner institutions understand the expectations of the program. Those research institutions range from large ones such as the

Philadelphia Free Library and the Historical Society of Pennsylvania, to smaller regional organizations, such as the Chestnut Hill Historical Society, or the Germantown Historical Society. They also include special collections, such as the Quaker Collection of Haverford College Library and the Charles Blockson African American Collection at Temple University, and historic sites, such as the Independence National Historical Park and the Mother Bethel African Methodist Episcopal Church.

Before the research process begins, students are given a substantial handout that details the project, their responsibilities, and the specific research institutions with which we are working. Each institution is given a listing like the following one:

HISTORICAL SOCIETY OF PENNSYLVANIA
1300 Locust Street, Philadelphia, PA, 19107
(215) 732-6200

Website:	www.libertynet.org/pahist
Hours:	Tuesdays, Thursday through Saturday: 10:00 am to 5:00 pm Wednesdays: 1:00 to 9:00 pm
Contact Person:	Sharon Ann Holt
Admission fee:	$2.00
Xeroxing:	.25 per copy (letter and legal size)
Holdings:	Archives of 8,000+ bound volumes of newspapers, church records, extensive genealogical and historical collections, maps, prints, and drawings. Valuable collections on prominent Philadelphians.

Students are directed to phone ahead and schedule a time for their visit as well as to inform the contact person of their topic. When visiting a library, collection, or historical site, students are asked to keep three things in mind: (1) "Rome wasn't built in a day and neither will your research be completed!" If they go to a library with the intention of zooming in and back out, they are wasting the staff's time as well as their own. They should plan to spend some quality time there (1.5 to 3 hours); (2) "There's no such thing as a free lunch . . . unless you eat at home (and even then, you're expected to take out the trash!)" Most of these institutions will charge a fee to use their collections. Since they are nonprofit organizations, the fees allow them to remain open to the general public. Often the entrance fee is no more than $3 with a student identification card. But even if this presents some difficulty, students may want to preview the holdings of a special collection on the institution's website and minimize the actual time spent at the site searching for materials. In this way, students can also limit the expense; and (3) "Document, Document, DOCUMENT!" Not only will students have to keep a detailed journal of the libraries, historical societies, and special collections they visit, but plan to take along a packet of 3″ × 5″ note cards to take notes on the various primary source documents they find.

I have found that these instructions limit the degree of student misunderstanding as well as teach young people the importance of stewardship of our cultural resources. Students also come to appreciate the fact that they are doing the work of a professional historian and that the experience will give them an advantage when they matriculate to college where these kinds of research papers will become more common.

The number of institutions visited by students varies, depending on their motivation. About four to six visits, some of which are repeat visits, are necessary to complete a quality research paper. The most highly motivated students do as many as double that amount.

Topic Selection

Because the research paper is a semester-long process and there are some fairly rigid demands on the students, it is imperative that students have some sense of ownership. That is why it is important for them to choose their own topic. They will be living with that topic for fourteen weeks; it's not like a high school romance, which routinely lasts about two weeks! Students must be certain that the topic complements their own interests, whether they be in politics, entertainment, sports, or the arts. If not, this will be one of the most painfully frustrating experiences they've ever had. Here are a variety of topics my students have done over the years:

Colonial Period, 1681–1765
Georgian style architecture; Chippendale furniture; founding of various denominational churches; natural history of the region; William Penn's founding of Philadelphia; establishment of earliest schools in the city; Quaker merchants and the slave trade; the beginnings of the abolitionist movement; treaties between the Penn family and the Delaware Indians; runaway slaves in colonial Philadelphia; boundary disputes between William Penn and Maryland's Lord Baltimore; impact of the French-Indian War on Philadelphia; political and religious symbolism of the Liberty Bell; comparing Penn's 1682 *Frame of Government* with the 1701 *Charter of Privileges*.

Revolutionary Period, 1765–1783

British occupation of Philadelphia; Battle of Germantown; Betsy Ross and the folklore of the first American flag; slaveholders in the Second Continental Congress; tavern culture; Benjamin Franklin, editor of the *Pennsylvania Gazette;* impact of Tom Paine's pamphlet, "Common Sense," on Philadelphia; Quaker response to war; the Philadelphia "Tea Party"; abridgement of civil liberties during wartime; mob violence in Philadelphia; response to the Stamp Act crisis of 1765; overthrowing the colonial constitution.

Early Republic, 1786–1820

How Philadelphia became the capital; proceedings of the Federal Convention of 1787; social life of the capital city; impact of Alexander Hamilton's First Bank on Philadelphia; James Madison courts Dolly; newspaper wars between Federalist and Democratic-Republican press; Yellow Fever epidemic drives President Washington out of the city; Federalist-style architecture; birth of the African Methodist Episcopal Church; founding of the Protestant Episcopal Church of the United States; Stephen Girard's Bank; physical expansion of the city; Charles W. Peale's Natural Science Museum—first of its kind; impact of Alien and Sedition Acts on Philadelphia.

Jacksonian and Antebellum Periods, 1828–1860

Impact of the Second Bank of the United States on Philadelphia's economy; Fairmount Waterworks, one of the city's first public utilities; Eastern State Penitentiary and prison reform; Lucretia Mott and the activities of the Philadelphia Female Anti-Slavery Society; Greek Revival Architecture and the contributions of William Strickland; textile mills of Manayunk; Frankford Arsenal mobilizes for the Civil War; cholera epidemic of 1832; Philadelphia establishes the first common school system in the state; burning of Pennsylvania Hall; Lafayette names the Pennsylvania State House, "Independence Hall"; Edwin Forrest and theater in Philadelphia; Philadelphia's railroad; the mansions of Fairmount Park; prominent residents of Laurel Hill Cemetery; Philadelphia's statuary; Jefferson Medical College and Hospital.

Civil War and Reconstruction, 1861–1876

Victorian architecture; Abraham Lincoln's inspirational visit to Independence Hall; Baldwin locomotives; political influence of Philadelphia's press; recruitment efforts in the city; Sgt. William Carney, flag bearer for the 54th Massachusetts; General George McClellan's Philadelphia roots; Camp William Penn and the training of

U.S. Colored Troops; Centennial Celebration of 1876; establishment of the city's parochial school system.

Industrial Era, 1877–1910

Professional baseball comes to Philadelphia; the building of City Hall; Boies Penrose, Bossism, and the birth of a corrupt Republican party machine; W. E. B. DuBois researches the Philadelphia Negro; Northern Liberties a melting pot of immigrant groups; Reading Terminal Market; Alexander Milne Calder and the making of the William Penn statue for City Hall; Negro League Baseball's Hilldales capture championship; Connie Mack and the Philadelphia Athletics create the first sporting dynasty; Haverford College, superpower of college soccer.

Twentieth Century

American Friends Service Committee, a Philadelphia-born institution with international impact; building of first skyskrapers; Franklin Institute; Philadelphia Art Museum; Boathouse Row; lifestyle in a rowhouse community; Great Depression's impact on the city; mass demotion of nineteenth-century buildings to create Independence National Historical Park; redevelopment of low-income districts into Society Hill section of the city; growth of commuter suburbs; Grace Kelly, a Philadelphia-born actress turned princess; Philadelphia's Navy Yard and mobilizing for World Wars; Eugene Ormandy and the Philadelphia Orchestra; Frank Rizzo, tough cop turned mayor; John Wanamaker, Philadelphia's most innovative retailer; Reverend Leon H. Sullivan and Progress Plaza, the city's first black-owned and operated shopping center; Dick Clark's American Bandstand and a rock 'n' roll revolution; 1978 MOVE confrontation with city police; Cecil B. Moore and the Philadelphia NAACP; desegregation of Girard College.

Of course, the topic must be "doable." That is, it cannot be too narrow in focus or there will not be sufficient information available. Nor can it be so broad that a six-page paper cannot do it justice. The above-mentioned topics are, in this sense, very doable in the time appropriated for such a project.

Students can get ideas for topics by combing through some general histories of their town or city. My students used two standard sources: Russell Weigley, editor, *Philadelphia: A 300-Year History*. (New York: W.W. Norton, 1982); and Edwin Wolf, *Philadelphia: Portrait of an American City* (Philadelphia: Camino Books, 1990). Both of these secondary sources organize Philadelphia's history by era and give a substantial survey of the social, political, economic, and cultural history of the city.

Next I have the students complete a topic selection form. The following form was completed by a student who wrote his research paper on Dick Clark's

American Bandstand, which began at WFIL Studios in West Philadelphia during the 1950s.

TOPIC SELECTION FORM

Subject of Study:	American Bandstand
Basic Information Gathering:	Philadelphia Free Library, Chestnut Hill Library
Question to be explored:	"How did American Bandstand affect youth culture in general and race relations in particular?"
Useful Data:	*Secondary source(s):*
	John Jackson, *American Bandstand: Dick Clark and the Making of a Rock 'n' Roll Empire.* New York: Oxford University, 1997.
	Primary source(s):
	Dick Clark with Fred Bronson. *Dick Clark's American Bandstand.* New York: Harper Collins, 1997.
	Interview with Myrna Horowitz, American Bandstand dancer: January 31, 1998.
Topic Headings / Subheadings:	Thesis; Philadelphia history; breaking color barrier; youth culture; integration; rhythm and blues artists.

The purpose of the topic selection form is twofold: to find out if the resources actually exist to complete a research paper on the subject; and to encourage students to think more critically about their topic than would be the case if they simply did some general background reading on it. The questions they formulate may lead to a thesis statement, which would be the answers to those questions. On the other hand, the questions may change as more research is completed. I also want students to begin thinking about organizing their papers by identifying some possible topic headings and subheadings. This will make it easier for them to organize their information as they are gathering it and allow them to make the transition to a working outline.

The Process of Writing a Research Paper

Completing the topic selection is only the first step in the process, though. Figure 2–2 illustrates the steps that lie ahead. This schematic diagram reinforces the importance of the process by showing the students all of the stages that are

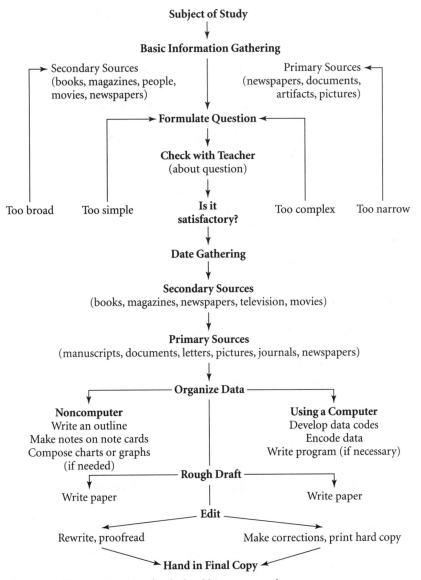

Figure 2–2. *Process of writing for the local history research paper*

involved in the research and writing of their papers. They become "detectives," using the evidence found in both primary and secondary sources to "solve their particular case." Like a detective, the evidence may lead them away from their initial hypothesis. If so, they can consult with the teacher, then return to the source materials to build a new, stronger case. After the data have been collected and a thesis determined, it is time to organize the data.

The word processor, which was not a staple of high school education when I began teaching in the early 1980s, provides students with a wonderful advantage these days. The "cut and paste" operation alone is worth the price of the computer. These days, some students even have laptop computers that they can take with them to a library and special collection, and complete their note taking directly onto the hard drive. Since not all students have access to a computer at home, however, I made sure that the process allowed for a typewritten paper as well. Regardless of the approach, all students must learn how to take notes when doing their research.

Note Taking

Research usually begins with a supply of 3″ × 5″ note cards that will be used to take down information from both primary and secondary sources relevant to the subject. One of the first obstacles a student faces is how to determine what kind of information is important. At the outset, I encourage students to learn as much as possible about the person, place, or events they are exploring by considering the following questions:

1. What is the time period of the subject?
2. What great events were occurring in American history at the time?
3. What is the relationship of the subject to the local community?
4. What is the significance of the subject to the local community, state, and/or nation?

These questions give the students a framework in which they can gather information and, later, organize that information into an outline. At that point, I am able to offer feedback, suggesting what areas need more research.

Another common frustration for students is deciding what information should be quoted or paraphrased. Although specific directions are not possible, I urge my students to consider the following points. First, is the author's phrasing particularly effective and/or precise? If so, use it. For example, many who watched American Bandstand during the period 1957 to 1989 will recall that Dick Clark signed off each show with the following farewell: "American Bandstand. It's got a great beat, and it's easy to dance to. Thanks for watching.

For now, this is Dick Clark . . . so long." Because of the popular appeal of the show and the unique way in which the farewell described American Bandstand, this is information that should be quoted.

Second, students should consider the length of the quotation. Only use those parts that are absolutely necessary to prove the point. The integration of quotation fragments into an argument rather than the use of block quotations is preferred because it demonstrates the student's understanding of the quote and how that particular piece of evidence supports the argument. For example, Dick Clark gave the following response when asked about his decision to integrate American Bandstand in 1957:

> One important change we made in 1957 was to introduce a lot of black musical talent to white America. I imagined that since the show was so highly visible and seen by so many millions of people, the idea of integration simply crept into society. There was no overt statement, no headline grabbing, no trumpets blaring—it just happened. And that was probably the best way for it to occur. I certainly didn't think of myself as a hero or a civil rights activist for integrating the show; it was just the right thing to do.[8]

The same statement can be delivered more effectively in the following manner:

> When Dick Clark integrated American Bandstand in 1957, there was no "headline grabbing." Nor did he consider himself a "hero or civil rights activist." Instead, he downplayed the event stating simply that "it was just the right thing to do."

Finally, I instruct my students that a failure to acknowledge the findings of another person (especially if those findings have only recently come to light), conflicting information (i.e., differing interpretations of a topic, dates, or statistics), ideas that can be traced to another historian, and direct quotation of a person, is literary theft, or plagiarism. When plagiarism occurs, it is treated as a major offense against the standards of academic honesty. Punishment can range from redoing the paper to a failing grade, depending on the severity of the offense. Colleges and secondary schools have been known to expel students for this offense as well. Deliberate plagiarism is, however, relatively rare. Most of what appears to be plagiarism in student work is unintentional borrowing, a result of inexperience, of carelessness in note taking, and of uncertainty as to the degree of documentation expected. The general rule for my students is: "If in doubt, footnote!"

When taking notes I instruct students to place a heading on each $3'' \times 5''$ note card with an indicator for book (B), primary source document (D), article (A), or interview (I) in the upper-righthand corner. Since they should already have a bibliography, which includes author, title, and all other relevant information of the sources being used, they need only to distinguish one book or article from another (i.e., A1, A2, A3, for articles / B1, B2, B3 for books, etc.). Students are asked to take only one note on each card so the outlining and writing process will go more smoothly. Time spent carefully taking notes saves time in these later stages. For example, say a student quotes or paraphrases sixteen separate times from the same book and places all of these references on three cards. When settling down to write the paper, he or she won't want to use this information in the same order, or even consecutively. If one idea is placed on one card, on the other hand, the student can organize the information more effectively when constructing the outline and the paper. Students should also avoid abbreviations when note taking. Abbreviations often result in confusion. Finally, each note card should have a subject label, or a brief descriptive phrase that indicates the heading and subheading on each card. Again, this method will save time and limit frustration when completing the outline. Here is the outline for the American Bandstand paper:

"American Bandstand: A Revolution in the Guise of a Television Show"

I. Introduction

    A: Opening: In the 1950s a small television show in South Philadelphia began broadcasting a conceptually new television idea. The show, "American Bandstand," was a dance show that broadcasted the latest music with regular and guest dancers. This was not an ordinary show, though.

    B: Thesis: American Bandstand became a revolution for both Philadelphia and the rest of the nation for three reasons: the show created new racial standards by breaking the color barrier on TV; it promoted the careers of many Rock 'n' Roll and Rhythm and Blues stars, who otherwise might not have been successful; and it changed America socially by creating a unique teenage lifestyle.

II. Body Sections

    A: Historical Background

        1. Philadelphia in the 1950s

            a. tensions between adults of different races

            b. children more accepting of racial differences

            c. statistics on population growth of teens

        2. Music

            a. decline of big bands

            b. rise of jazz

            c. rise of rock 'n' roll and negative image

B: American Bandstand (cause of change)
1. integrated black dancers on show
2. promoted music of struggling artists
3. insisted on "clean cut" look of dancers

C: Effects of American Bandstand
1. promoted integration to a national television audience
2. gave failing artists a chance to rise to the top
3. popularized a new youth culture, making rock 'n' roll more acceptable for older generations

III. Conclusion

It's important to note that the above outline was the most detailed of three outlines that had been completed by the student during the process. I call the earlier outlines "working outlines" because they allow the student to think through the factual material and the mechanics of the paper before actually beginning to write. Again, the act of organizing this information either by hand or word processor is extremely important because it gives the students tangible products of their works.

Assessment of Two Research Papers

Now, let's examine each part of the outline as it has been developed in the final paper itself, beginning with the title. As previously mentioned, I want my students to create a two-part title that will address the general topic as well as identify the argument they intend to make. In this paper, the student's general topic is "American Bandstand." The particular argument he intends to make is reflected in the secondary title, "A Revolution in the Guise of a Television Show." This secondary title must be more clearly developed in the thesis statement, or the last two sentences of the introduction:

> **Introduction:** In the 1950s a small television show in South Philadelphia began broadcasting a conceptually new television idea. The show, "American Bandstand," was a dance show that broadcasted the latest music with regular and guest dancers. This was not an ordinary show, though.
>
> American Bandstand became a revolution for both Philadelphia and the rest of the nation for three reasons: the show created new racial standards by breaking the color barrier on TV; it promoted the careers of many Rock 'n' Roll and Rhythm and Blues stars, who otherwise might not have been successful; and it changed America socially by creating a unique teenage lifestyle.

The introduction opens with a statement that identifies the historical context of the paper and the general topic area. In this case, the student identifies "the 1950s" as the time period under investigation and "a new television idea" as the general topic. He narrows the focus of the introduction by identifying that "new television idea" as "American Bandstand," or a "dance show that broadcasted the latest music with regular and guest dancers." Now he is ready to state his thesis, specifically that American Bandstand "became a revolution for both Philadelphia and the rest of the nation." More important, he reveals three ways in which the show was revolutionary: (1) by creating "new racial standards" which "broke the color barrier on TV"; (2) by promoting "the careers of many Rock 'n' Roll and Rhythm and Blues stars, who otherwise might not have been successful"; and (3) by "creating a unique teenage lifestyle," which, in turn, "changed America socially." In addition, these three effects provide an organization for the argument. In other words, the reader can expect to see topic sentences in each body section that clarify each part of the thesis.

The topic sentence to the first body section should, in some way, clarify the historical context of American Bandstand and why the show was able to promote a revolutionary change in music and/or society for both Philadelphia and the nation. The topic sentence of the second body section should address the way in which American Bandstand was a catalyst for revolutionary change. Finally, the topic sentence of the third body section should address the effects on Philadelphia and the nation of this revolutionary change. Let's examine each body section individually to see how successful the student was in developing the argument.

Body Section 1: Philadelphia was not always the "City of Brotherly Love" back in the 1950s. It harbored a lot of racial prejudice and was the "northern-most southern city" in the nation.[1] There was racial tension in the air, but it was mainly the result of tensions among adults. Black and white children had very little trouble living together. Schools were integrated and there were very few problems between races in them.[2] However, the adults still lagged behind and did not copy their children's attitudes.

These attitudes also included the children's views on music. Rock 'n' Roll was the new hit after the "Big Band Era" of the 1920s through the 1940s. After the war, big bands were hard to fund and maintain. They disintegrated into smaller jazz quartets and trios and the "wall of sound" effect died away. Rock 'n' roll developed out of this small band setup by using electrical bases and guitars to present a new feel of music which emphasized different kinds of beats. This radical change did not sit well with the adults, who considered it a loud and obnoxious sound compared with the smooth, relaxed tones of the jazz era. Consequently, adults called rock 'n' roll "the devil's music, and a scourge on the nation's youth."[3] Rock was also viewed as black music that "encouraged delinquency, sex, drugs and protests."[4]

The 1950s was a time of tension between generations. World War II was over, and a wave of "baby boomers" was reaching the dreaded teen years. In 1950, children ages 10 to 14 were 6.4% of the population, while teens ages 15 to 19 were 6.2% of the population. By 1959 those numbers had grown to 9.3% and 7.3%, respectively. While these may not seem like large percentage increases, the actual numbers were significantly larger. Of the 10- to 14-year-old group, there was an increase of 7.1 million, and an increase of 3.6 million teens for the 15- to 19-year-old group. In comparison to adults ages 20 to 24 (an increase of 983,000 during the same decade) and adults ages 25 to 29 (an increase of 113,000), the population growth of teenagers was much more significant.[5]

Because a large percentage of the general population were teenagers, there was a rise in sex, delinquency, fast cars, and motorcycles, which come naturally at this age. Parents, offended by the idea that these unwanted behaviors were on the rise, discouraged what they believed was the cause of them. In fact, there was really no change in the type of teenage behavior, only that there were more numbers of kids participating in them. Many adults pointed to rock 'n' roll music as the main cause.

Children, too, were affected by the rise in rebellious acts. Teens began getting more media coverage and their behavior began to influence other teens and even preteens. The beginnings of television increased the desire for media exposure. Soon, everyone wanted to be on TV. Teens achieved this goal by causing trouble. Then, in 1952, American Bandstand began and teenagers were given the opportunity to gain more positive media coverage.

Endnotes:

1. Interview of Dick Clark, West Philadelphia: September 10, 1997.

2. Interview of Myrna Horowitz, Philadelphia: January 31, 1998.

3. Dick Clark with Michael Shore, *The History of American Bandstand: It's Got A Great Beat and You Can Dance to It.* (New York: Baltimore Books, 1985), 13.

4. Clark interview.

5. Philadelphia Bulletin, *Almanac and Yearbook.* (Philadelphia: The Philadelphia Evening Bulletin, 1960), 192.

This body section opens with the topic sentence: "Philadelphia was not always the 'City of Brotherly Love' back in the 1950s." Although the sentence does give the reader an historical context for the paper and suggests that the student will discuss the social history of Philadelphia in the 1950s, it does not address American Bandstand, or how the show might have emerged as a result of this environment. A better topic sentence for this section might have been: "The origins of American Bandstand can be traced to the racial and generational conflicts that were taking place in Philadelphia in the 1950s." This sentence also identifies historical context, but, more important, it clarifies the nature of the social conflicts out of which American Bandstand grew. Such a clarification is important because of the student's decision to emphasize generational and racial differences and how the show navigated those differences.

If we turn to the substantive argument, we can see that this body section offers some keen insight and persuasive evidence. The argument that teen culture exercised a significant influence on society because of the sheer numbers of adolescents is a good one. As the student points out, there was nothing new to rebellious adolescent behavior, only that "there were more numbers of kids participating in them." He reinforces the point with some convincing statistical data on the population growth of adolescents during the decade of the 1950s.

Just as insightful is the anecdotal evidence he has culled from interviews with Myrna Horowitz, a regular dancer on the show, and Dick Clark himself. Not only did the student make these personal contacts, which is good, investigative research, but integrated their eyewitness accounts insightfully into his argument. Horowitz gives us testimony on the different approaches adults and children took towards race relations in the 1950s, suggesting that it was easier for youth to accept integration because they did not experience a history of racial conflict. On the other hand, this section would have been stronger had the student offered more detailed evidence on some of the racial tensions that existed among adults. I also question Horowitz's statement that the city's public schools were integrated.

I assume that her school was integrated, but that was certainly not the case for public schools in the rest of the city. Desegregation was a hotly contested process that occurred throughout the 1960s and 1970s in Philadelphia and not all of the conflict was created by the adults either.[9] I made this point to the student and left him with the decision on whether or not to revise the statement. Of course, he decided to keep her remarks intact because it not only served to prove his thesis, but because the interviewee earnestly believed them. Although I still contested the point in the grading of the final paper, it was more important that he be allowed to make an informed judgment on the evidence he collected and whether or not he could use it responsibly.

The student's integration of Dick Clark's memories were more insightful. Clark's remark that Philadelphia was the "northern-most southern city" in the nation is an important contextual statement of the 1950s, indicating his awareness of why racial conflict existed in the city at that time and suggesting that he understood the obstacle he was facing in integrating his show. Certainly the general perception among adults that rock music "encouraged delinquency, sex, drugs and protests" underscores the challenge Clark faced when he became host of the television dance show. Although I believe that this section would have been strengthened by including more of Philadelphia's social history, the eyewitness accounts not only offer direct

Figure 2–3. *Black teens first appeared on American Bandstand in
1957, though they had to dance in segregated couples.
(Photo Courtesy of Dick Clark Productions)*

evidence of the tenuous nature of race relations and rock music in 1950s
Philadelphia, but create a framework for the terms of the argument in the
second body section on how American Bandstand served as a catalyst for
revolutionary change.

Body Section 2: American Bandstand promoted integration, a younger generation of singers, and a more accepting, clean-cut youth culture. When Dick
Clark became the host of the show on July 9, 1956, he invited blacks to dance
on it.[6] He believed that blacks had made "a significant contribution to Rock 'n'
Roll and it was important to recognize that contribution."[7] The decision was a
revolutionary one. Before American Bandstand blacks had not been on television. In addition most of the dancers on the show, from its beginnings in 1952,
were of Italian descent.[8] While the black dancers got along well with the white
dancers, black and white couples danced separately as shown [in Figure 2–3].[9]
Not until the early 1970s did American Bandstand allow for inter-racial couples
to dance together.[10] Regardless of race, the teens seemed to enjoy the music
because Clark promoted both black and white artists.[11]

Figure 2–4. *Teens on American Bandstand were required to be clean-cut in appearance and well behaved.*
(Courtesy of Dick Clark Productions)

Many of these young musical artists were unknown. Some came in off the street into the studio. They were interviewed by Clark himself and played on the show. A few weeks later they became superstars when their song became a hit record. Frankie Avalon, one of these overnight stars, said that his "fan mail came into the television station by the thousands within a week of his appearance on the show." After his third appearance, he "couldn't just walk through the studio door anymore," he had to have a "police escort."[12]

Fabian, another musician, also claims that his music "would never have been big were it not for [his] exposure on American Bandstand."[13] Because the show had such a large television audience, these musicians were able to become stars overnight. A circular pattern developed: after the artist appeared on the show their record sales went up; kids who bought the record told their friends about it, who, in turn, also bought a record; as the record became more popular more kids would tune into the show to listen to the next big star. Soon, even the parents who had discouraged rock music were watching the show.[14]

Dick Clark's major accomplishment, however, was giving credibility to the new music and the young people who listened to it. He made American

Bandstand appealing to people of all ages. Integration inspired curiosity. People who might have never watched the show tuned in to see kids of different races dancing together in the same studio. Clark also invited disabled teens onto the dance floor. Myrna Horowitz, for example, had polio and was forced to wear a leg brace while she danced. But because she was such a good dancer she was accepted by the other teens.[15] Couples danced to set movements with the boys leading and the girls following.[16] [Figure 2–4] shows that all dancers, shown here sitting on bleachers and waiting for the show to begin, were clean-cut and had to follow a dress code. Girls were to wear dresses while the boys were required to wear sports jackets. Behavior was never discussed, but everyone realized that they were to be respectful of each other.[17]

Endnotes:

6. John Jackson, *American Bandstand: Dick Clark and the Making of a Rock and Roll Empire.* (New York: Oxford University Press, 1997), 35.

7. Clark interview.

8. Clark & Shore, *History of American Bandstand,* 7.

9. Photograph taken from Clark & Bronson, *Dick Clark's American Bandstand,* 112–13.

10. Ibid.

11. Clark interview.

12. Frankie Avalon quoted on Clark & Shore, *History of American Bandstand,* 29.

13. Fabian quoted in Clark & Shore, *History of American Bandstand,* 21.

14. Clark interview; Horowitz interview.

15. Horowitz interview.

16. Clark interview.

17. Photograph taken from Clark & Bronson, *Dick Clark's American Bandstand,* 56–57.

This second body section opens with the topic sentence: "American Bandstand promoted integration, a younger generation of singers, and a more accepting, clean-cut youth culture." The reader has a good idea of the argument and the order in which it will be presented. Accordingly, integration is the first topic addressed in this section. The student uses both primary and secondary source accounts to discuss the nature of integration and how it proceeded. He refrains from making the blanket statement that integration came full-blown to the show. Instead he is careful to draw the distinction between dancing by "segregated couples" and, later, in the 1970s, "inter-racial couples." He also includes a primary source photograph as evidence.

The second topic is the promotion of a younger generation of singers on the show. While the student offers the reader a concise explanation of the cyclical relationship between an appearance on American Bandstand and "overnight success," he is much less successful in making the transition to this topic from his earlier discussion on integration. To be sure, Dick Clark introduced white artists like Frankie Avalon and Fabian. But just as important—and more important to the process of integration—was his introduction of black artists like Chubby Checker, Johnny Mathis, and Little Richard. Some discussion of these artists would have strengthened this section of the paper in particular, and the case he is trying to make, in general.

The final topic in this body section is the promotion of a more accepting, clean-cut youth culture. Again, the student uses a primary source photograph to prove his point. The photograph is persuasive evidence because it not only shows the well-groomed appearance of the teens, but also the integrated nature of the show with the two black teens seated in the front row alongside other white females. Additionally, the student continues to draw evidence from the eyewitness accounts of Myrna Horowitz and Dick Clark in discussing the broad-based appeal of the show as well as the dress code and personal etiquette that was implicitly understood by the teenage dancers. Although this same point was made by Fred Bronson in *Dick Clark's American Bandstand*, I am more impressed with the student's interpretation.[10] Bronson concentrated on the acceptance of the show by adults because of the dress code and proper behavior of the teenagers. The student, on the other hand, brings the issue of physical disability into the discussion. While the inspiration for this point comes from the fact that one of the interviewees was disabled, he uses the case to show that some of the attraction of this younger, clean-cut generation was their acceptance of not only black contemporaries but those with disabilities as well.

Now that the second body section has set the stage for the effects of American Bandstand on American culture, let's move on to Body Section 3.

Body Section 3: American Bandstand exercised a tremendous influence on the nation by promoting integration to a national television audience, introducing new artists, and making rock 'n' roll more acceptable for American society. Integrating American Bandstand was an act of genius on the part of Dick Clark. He broadened his viewing audience to many young blacks who wanted to know if there were differences between their style of dancing and that of whites. There was also a large audience who wanted to see how blacks and whites would get along together on a dance floor. This was especially true in the southern states where segregation still existed.[18]

Figure 2–5. *Dick Clark, like the teens on his show, was also clean-cut and well mannered. Teens and artists were attracted by his friendly nature, considering him like a "big brother."*
(Courtesy of Dick Clark Productions)

New artists also began to emerge. With each new song, a new dance step seemed to be invented, and as the songs and dances became popular so did the recording artists. Bobby Rydell, Dion, Fredy Cannon, and Fats Domino rose to the top of the record charts.[19] Chubby Checker immortalized "the Twist" on the show, while others followed with dances like the "Calypso," "Bop," "Strand," "Mashed Potato," and the "Limbo."[20] All over America people saw and imitated these dances. But that was not all they imitated.

The regulars became incredibly popular. Teens idolized them and wanted to be just like them.[21] Girls copied their hairdos and their make-up, while boys copied their clothing and dance steps.[22] Some of the regulars were teased in school by teen-aged "bullies," probably because of jealousy. Clark supported them though. He would not allow any fighting inside the studio and cultivated clean-cut behavior as well as looks. By keeping out the "bad crowd" and insisting that all dancers be well groomed, Clark brought respectability to rock music and ensured that parents would approve of it. He also made sure that all musicians who appeared on the show followed the same rules and, as shown [in Figure 2–5], he set an example in his own personal behavior and appearance.[23]

The dancers and the artists followed his lead because he appealed to them. Clark spoke to them at their own level, being careful not to patronize them or distance himself from them as a celebrity. According to Myrna Horowitz, "everyone felt like they knew him like a brother."[24]

Endnotes:

18. Clark interview.

19. Ibid.

20. Clark & Shore, *History of American Bandstand,* 75.

21. Horowitz interview.

22. Clark & Shore, *History of American Bandstand,* 75.

23. Photograph taken from Clark & Bronson, *Dick Clark's American Bandstand,* 52–53.

24. Horowitz interview.

The third body section begins with the topic sentence: "American Bandstand exercised a tremendous influence on the nation by promoting integration to a national television audience, introducing new artists, and making rock 'n' roll more acceptable for American society." The sentence previews the organization of the section, allowing the reader to anticipate the three issues that will be discussed in it. Like the other body sections, the mechanics of the writing, particularly the integration of primary source quotes and the transitions made between the various sections, give coherence to the paper. The difficulty with this particular section is the lack of evidence to support the case that American Bandstand had, indeed, a national impact.

With the exception of the photograph, all of the evidence is anecdotal, coming from personal accounts and, in particular, from Dick Clark himself. Even the book that is cited in the endnotes is co-authored by Clark. This section would have been stronger if the student presented more objective, secondary sources. For example, John Jackson's *American Bandstand: Dick Clark and the Making of a Rock and Roll Empire,* which the student cited earlier in his paper, is highly critical of Clark's motives and raises serious questions about the degree to which American Bandstand had as great an impact on youth culture as other writers have suggested. Similarly, the student might have used secondary sources that surveyed the popular culture and, specifically, musical culture of the 1950s to prove his point.[11] If nothing else, he should have mentioned that American Bandstand was so popular across the nation by 1964 the show had relocated to California, and by 1989 when the last show was broadcasted across the nation, American Bandstand held the distinction of being television's longest running and most popular dance program in history.[12]

Finally, the student must summarize the main points of his argument in a brief conclusion and offer an insight that will place the significance of the topic in the broader context of U.S. history and/or current events.

> **Conclusion:** American Bandstand was indeed a revolution that hid under the guise of a TV show. Clark broke the color barrier by integrating black dancers into the show. He promoted many musicians that would never have made it were they not on the show. In turn, the musicians introduced new dances that became popular. He changed the way teenagers acted and dressed by having the regulars set a good example. Most important, he made rock 'n' roll acceptable to many who had previously scorned it by making American Bandstand an attractive, wholesome environment. American Bandstand made Dick Clark famous. But did Clark make the show famous?
>
> Clark was the right person in the right place at the right time. The baby boom generation was just reaching their adolescence when the show began and teenagers wanted greater media exposure. TV also became more common in homes across the country, giving them that kind of exposure. The 1950s was also a time when integration and new musical styles were being tested. Clark recognized all of these things and capitalized on them in a way that was acceptable to both the young generation and their parents' generation. Ultimately, Clark's achievement was American Bandstand's as well.

This is a very strong conclusion because it summarizes clearly and concisely the major points of the argument and, more importantly, placed both Clark and American Bandstand in the larger context of America's music history. I like that the student recognizes the reciprocal influence of Clark and the dance show. In this way, he demonstrates his understanding of the complexity of history, specifically that there is an intimate connection between individuals and movements. Had Clark not been the host of American Bandstand, someone else might have assumed the same role in breaking down the color barrier and making youth culture more acceptable to younger generations. But the fact is that Clark was the person to do it. His success allowed American Bandstand to influence the youth of the 1950s. At the same time, his efforts were successful because of the times. As the student points out, the baby boom generation was reaching adolescence, integration was one of the most pressing issues in society, and rock music appealed to both black and white teens. Without those trends, Clark and American Bandstand would not have enjoyed a national appeal.

Finally, the annotated bibliography identifies the six sources that were consulted as well as their value to the paper. According to the research paper requirements, there must be five bibliographic sources, three of which must be primary sources. In this paper, four of the six sources are primary, demonstrating that the student took seriously the investigative responsibilities of an historian.

ANNOTATED BIBLIOGRAPHY

Clark, Dick. Interview, West Philadelphia: September 10, 1997.
Most valuable source containing Clarks' reflections in his years as host of American Bandstand.
Clark, Dick and Fred Bronson. *Dick Clark's American Bandstand*. NY: Harper-Collins, 1997.
Important source for firsthand accounts on the show, its dancers and artists. Used throughout the paper.
Horowitz, Myrna. Interview, Philadelphia: January 31, 1998.
Another important source for firsthand information by a regular dancer on the show. Used throughout the paper.
Jackson, John. *American Bandstand: Dick Clark and the Making of a Rock and Roll Empire*. New York: Oxford University Press, 1997.
Shows another, less attractive side of American Bandstand. Jackson is critical of Clark's motives for hosting the show. Sees him as egocentric. This source provides a competing perspective.
Philadelphia Bulletin, *Almanac and Yearbook*. Phila.: The Evening Bulletin, 1960.
Good source for statistics on the baby boom generation and U.S. population growth, which helped in writing of the historical background section.
Shore, Michael with Dick Clark. *The History of American Bandstand*. N.Y.: Ballantine, 1985.
Primarily written by Shore with interview material from Clark. This source offers an objective account of the show, particularly on the subjects of integration and youth culture.

In terms of creativity, this paper is first-rate. The student went to great lengths to secure eyewitness accounts, integrated those accounts persuasively into his argument, framed the topic in the broader context of American popular culture, and left the reader with an important insight about the reciprocal influence of the individual and an historical movement. Less successful was the proof of the argument, which was based primarily on anecdotal rather than factual evidence. Remember, however, that the local history research paper is a process. The student was graded on seven different criteria which totaled 100 points. While the final paper received the equivalent of a "B" for the reasons just mentioned, the student's diligence over the fourteen weeks of the assignment allowed him to earn an "A—" for the project. That is, the cumulative number of points he earned for all grading criterion totaled a 92 or an "A—."

In addition to my evaluation, I require that all students do a peer evaluation of another student's first draft. The process has proven to be a valuable one. Not only does it give the student a basis of comparison for his own work, but can often motivate him to be more careful in writing the final draft. Each student is given a peer evaluation form and is graded on the degree to which he offers a constructive analysis and advice of a peer's paper. The form is similar to a rubric in that it signals all the criteria upon which the paper will be evaluated. However, I do not offer specific examples of what constitutes an "outstanding," "above average," "average," or "below average" paper. My experience with rubrics has taught me that they discourage creativity on the part of the student and handcuff me as an evaluator of student work. Too often students—and sometimes parents—appeal for a higher grade using the rubric as a defense. Since my goal is to develop students as writers and not "grade grubbers," I use peer evaluations, rather than rubrics, as a method of assessment.[13]

Peer Evaluation

NOTE: *The reviewer is to provide constructive commentary on the paper being considered. Remember, only honest, candid remarks will benefit the writer. Be as thorough as possible.*

Name of Reviewer: _____

Name of Writer: _____

Title of Paper: _____

Thesis Statement (Identify the thesis as you understand it):
Can the thesis statement be clearly identified? Is it located in the proper place? Is it provable?

Organization: Do the topic sentences preview the paragraphs that follow? Do the topic sentences develop the thesis? Is the paper organized by key ideas? Are transitions between key ideas made smoothly?

Mechanical Skills: Is there a clear sentence construction? Any "run-on" sentences or "run-on" paragraphs? Punctuation problems? Problems with grammar or spelling? Proper endnoting? Proper bibliographic form? (Be sure to note all problems for the writer.)

Development of Argument: Does the writer provide sufficient factual evidence to support his argument? Is there a balance of concept, fact, and explanation in the paper? Is the argument a creative one? Do you believe the argument, as stated in the thesis, has been proven?

Bibliographic Sources: Are there a minimum of five sources used? Are there at least three primary sources? Is there at least one general history used? Are all the sources listed in the bibliography actually used in the paper? (Check endnotes for verification.)

The American Bandstand paper is a good example of the kind of creativity a student can bring to the research and writing process if given ownership of it. This particular student would not have been as successful had he been forced to select a more traditional topic. Post-World War II popular culture and music, in particular, are the topics that interested him. However, there have also been students who chose to research earlier time periods and did some exceptionally creative work as well. Although I will not repeat, step-by-step, the research and writing processes for these papers, I think it might be valuable for you to get an overview of some other research papers I found to be particularly interesting.

Institutional histories, though more traditional in nature, are often subject matter for students. Too often, however, a student will want to address the entire history of an institution. Some have proposed such daunting topics as "Independence Hall," and "The American Philosophical Society." These topics are, of course, unrealistic for a six- to eight-page research paper. I convinced the student who wanted to write on Independence Hall that a more doable topic would be a specific event that occurred there. She chose to explore the Federal Convention of 1787 and eventually narrowed her focus to the social life of the delegates during the convention. Her paper examined the banquets and dances they attended in the city as well as their enjoyment of Philadelphia's cultural life at the time. Similarly, the student who wrote on the American Philosophical Society eventually narrowed his focus to Benjamin Franklin's involvement in the founding of that institution and his vision of lifelong learning for adults.

Other students are more focused. One of the more fascinating papers I read addressed our school's history. Because Penn Charter was founded in 1689 by the English Quaker William Penn and was, for most of the eighteenth and early nineteenth centuries, the most prestigious school in Philadelphia, its history is synonymous with that of the city. This particular student was interested in researching the impact of the War for American Independence on Penn Charter, then known as "The Friends Public School." Inspired by the fact that the Religious Society of Friends, or Quakers, who ran the school were devout pacifists, he wanted to know how American patriots, as well as the British Army during their occupation of Philadelphia, treated both the school and its teachers. Here's the opening paragraph of "The Friends Public School: A Quaker Institution at War":

> At the height of the American Revolution, an exasperated John Adams was asked to offer his impression of Philadelphia's Quakers. "They are dull as beetles," he snapped, "a neutral tribe, a race of the insipid from who neither good is to be expected nor evil to be apprehended." Adams' ire was inspired by the Quakers' neutral stance in the American Revolution. Having withdrawn from the larger secular society they helped to establish, Philadelphia Friends watched

the battles of the American Revolution from behind their windows. It must have been a frustrating vantage point, but it was one they believed absolutely necessary for the survival of their faith and the Quaker institutions their forefathers had established.

What impresses me about this opening paragraph is the conciseness and creativity with which the student poses the Quaker dilemma. Not only does he juxtapose the Friends' religiously inspired neutrality to the war against the frustration of John Adams, the motivating force of American independence, but he does so with a graphic quote that immediately captures the reader's interest. If I am the reader, I want to know more: "Why did Quakers withdraw from the secular society?" "What about their faith inspired neutrality?" "Is Adams' reaction common among the other founding fathers, or unique to him?" The student has peaked my curiosity about all of these issues.

The next few paragraphs narrow the focus of the introduction to the Friends Public School, its mission as defined by William Penn (i.e., to cultivate and ensure the practice of Quaker ideals in the larger society), and the Overseers who became the stewards of the school. Then, he asks an important question of his own, and one that provides a nice framework for the thesis statement:

> The American Revolution posed a critical dilemma for the Quakers who were charged with the oversight of the Friends Public School. Should they follow William Penn's belief in pacifism and risk the destruction of an educational institution which represented that belief, or defend the liberty of conscience that Penn made the cornerstone of his New World colony and betray their religion's peaceable principles? In short, these Friends were being forced to choose between loyalty to their colony and loyalty to their faith.
>
> While some Quakers actively supported the patriot cause, the Overseers of the Friends Public School, like the majority of the Society of Friends, remained neutral in accordance with the Peace Testimony. Most divorced themselves from political society and assumed an unaccustomed isolationism. In so doing, they not only earned the wrath of the American patriots, but jeopardized the welfare of the Friends public school.

By now you can see that this young man possesses an impressive vocabulary and a gift for literary expression. He has made very clear the specific dilemma of the Overseers: "Which of Penn's principles do they follow—pacifism or liberty of conscience?" The American Revolution is forcing the choice because of the patriot's unconditional commitment to the latter principle. The thesis informs us that there was a divided response. Some

Quakers chose to support the movement for American independence, others, like the Overseers, did not; and they suffered for it. As the argument unfolds, the student details, with both primary and secondary sources, the depredations committed against the Overseers and their Friends Public School by their patriot neighbors as well as the Continental and Redcoat armies. Accused of being "Tories" or "British sympathizers" for refusing to take an oath of loyalty to the new United States government, many of the Overseers were charged with being "notoriously disaffected," arrested, and "held without trial in the Walnut Street jail." Others were exiled to Winchester, Virginia, so they could not "stir up any trouble." The Redcoats were not much better in their treatment of the Overseers and their school. During the British occupation of Philadelphia in the winter of 1777–1778, the Redcoat Army enforced a Quartering Act, which directed all citizens to house a soldier upon request. When one of the Overseers refused, an angry Redcoat "drew his sword and split the door into pieces." In addition, the Friends Public School was taken over by British troops on Christmas Day and "rampant pillaging occurred." Shortly after, the Overseers were forced to shut the school down for five months, until the British left the city. The last body section addresses how the Overseers responded to the harassment:

> Because students and Overseers wrote very little on the subject, it is difficult to determine exactly how they responded to this harassment. However, the *Friends Public School Gazette,* the first student newspaper printed in the United States, provides some clues. While the editorials express the views of a small body of students at best, they reveal some mixed emotions. It is clear that the students took an interest in political matters, since the paper contains periodic updates on local elections and, in a 1777 issue, states that it is the "duty of the Friends Public School to support the American government."
>
> In a more revealing editorial that same year, an insightful student asks his peers to consider the formation of a separate nation if the Anglo-American conflict should lead to civil war, particularly when the war itself contradicts the fundamental principles of their Quaker religion. He concludes by suggesting that it would not be wise to support the Revolutionary cause but rather to "stand by the articles of our Quaker faith." Another editorial warns of the physical brutality of war, suggesting that "honor and glory" may not be worth the price of "life and limb." Essentially, these student-writers favored the creation of a new and independent nation, but they were reluctant to offer their unconditional support in fighting for it.
>
> While the students debated, the Overseers maintained a conspicuous silence. There is no mention of anger, frustration, or support for either side in

their monthly meeting minutes. This was done intentionally. Any document stating such emotions or revealing internal disagreements would be viewed as a sign that the Quaker community was abandoning neutrality. Overseers, like the majority of Friends, formed a separate society. They withdrew from their positions in the Pennsylvania government and ordered their schools to teach only the "children of Friends," so that greater care "may be taken regarding their conduct and religious instruction."

The Overseers felt that this action was necessary in order to uphold their testimony on peace, and never expressed an opinion for or against the war in public. Therefore, it is difficult to know with any certainty how they felt about the British, who stormed their schools, or the Americans, who harassed and arrested them without probable cause.

Throughout this section, the student is extremely responsible in the use of the primary sources at his disposal. He is careful not to make sweeping statements, but rather to distinguish the feelings of those students who actually wrote about the war from the majority who did not. He also makes an important distinction between the personal journals and correspondence of the Overseers, which are extensively quoted in the earlier sections of the paper, and their monthly meeting minutes, which serve as the official records of the Friends Public School. In fact, this paper reflects the most responsible—and extensive—use of primary source documentation of any high school research paper that I have read. Not only did the student make use of documents from Penn Charter's archives, such as the *Minutes of the Overseers, 1698–1783* and the *Friends Public School Gazette,* but he made many trips to the special collections of the Historical Society of Pennsylvania and the Quaker Collection of Haverford College Library in order to research the personal correspondence of many Overseers as well as the *Minutes of Philadelphia Monthly Meeting.*

Together with the quality of the student's writing and the fact that no secondary interpretation of the Friends Public School during the American Revolution existed at the time, this work was the most exceptional piece of student writing that I had seen.[14] I encouraged the student to make some minor revisions and submit it for publication in *The Concord Review,* a quarterly journal devoted to the publication of high school history essays. Since 1987, *The Concord Review* has published more than 500 high school history papers by students from forty-two states and thirty-three other countries. Essays of approximately 5,000 words (with endnotes and bibliography) on any historical topic (ancient, foreign, or domestic) may be submitted.[15] I am proud to claim that *The Concord Review* accepted this essay and it appeared in the Fall 1994 issue of that publication.[16]

Summary

Position papers and the local history research paper are wonderful ways of teaching the fundamental skills of the discipline of history: to think, read, and write in a critical fashion. They also develop quite naturally from the earlier documentary analyses discussed in Part One. At the same time, these forms of writing teach students that writing is, indeed, a process that takes place over weeks, even months. The position paper is often the final product of two to three weeks of study of a particular issue. Insights from class discussion, notes from lectures as well as assigned readings, and even information from educational or commercial videos on an historical topic can be integrated into the argument. The local history research paper further underscores the process of writing by making students accountable for a series of assignments that, if completed carefully, should culminate in a quality piece of writing.

But what about less traditional approaches? How can a teacher appeal to the multiple intelligences of students as a method of historical inquiry? What specific exercises, personal challenges, and class projects will make the study of history meaningful and personally relevant to their own lives? These are the subject matter for Part Three.

Endnotes

1. The integration of social sciences into the discipline of history have forced professional historians to reconsider the ways in which they write as well. The turgid, pompous, and obscure prose that once passed for "historical scholarship" have been replaced with more lucid and insightful sociological analysis. One of the finest books to address this development as well as the integration of the social sciences into the writing process is Howard S. Becker and Pamela Richards, *Writing for Social Scientists. How to Start and Finish Your Thesis, Book, or Article.* (Chicago: University of Chicago, 1986).

2. Writing is not a special gift like art or music. A student can learn to write well if he understands the steps involved in the process. This is true for writing in any subject area, not just history. William Zinsser in his best-selling book, *On Writing Well. The Classic Guide to Writing Nonfiction* (New York: Harper Collins, 1998, seventh edition), offers some wonderful insights into the principles, methods, and various forms of writing nonfiction.

3. See Paul K. Conkin, *The New Deal.* (Arlington Heights, Illinois: Harlan Davidson, 1975), 67–78; William E. Leuchtenburg. *Franklin D. Roosevelt and the New Deal, 1932–1940.* (New York: Harper & Row, 1963), 326–48; James MacGregor Burns, *Roosevelt: The Lion and the Fox, 1882–1940.* (New York: Harcourt Brace Jovanovich,

1956), 328–36; and Dexter Perkins, *The New Age of Franklin Roosevelt, 1932–45.* (Chicago: University of Chicago, 1957), 58–80, 171–72.

4. The text I use for my U.S. History course is Gary B. Nash and Julie Roy Jeffrey, editors. *The American People. Creating a Nation and a Society.* (New York: Harper & Row, 1986).

5. See William E. Leuchtenberg, *In the Shadow of FDR. From Harry Truman to Ronald Reagan.* (Ithaca: Cornell University, 1983). Leuchtenberg explores the presidencies of Truman, Eisenhower, Kennedy, Johnson, Nixon, Ford, Carter, and Reagan to show how Franklin D. Roosevelt's legacy influenced both their domestic and foreign policies.

6. Student ownership of the local history research paper is critical to the success of the enterprise. I want my students to be active in their own educations, not passive bystanders. At the same time, I have a responsibility to cultivate student ownership, which I do through cooperative learning exercises and writing workshops. For example, each step of the research and writing process is preceded with a workshop on how to approach that particular assignment whether it be on choosing a topic, crafting an annotated bibliography, taking note-cards, or writing the rough draft of the paper. Students are asked to complete exercises like the ones I have already outlined in Part One. In this way, I encourage students to practice history just as the professionals. One of the best books on how to create an engaging history classroom through workshops is Cynthia Stokes Brown, *Connecting with the Past. History Workshop in Middle and High Schools.* (Portsmouth, NH: Heinemann, 1994).

7. See Kate L. Turabian, *A Manual for Writers of Term Papers, Theses, and Dissertations.* (Chicago: University of Chicago, 1982, fifth edition). Turabian is widely recognized as the standard resources for high school and college students. Based on *The Chicago Manual of Style,* Turabian's Manual for Writers offers comprehensive and detailed guidelines for the preparation of manuscripts, focusing on the needs of computer users.

8. Dick Clark quoted by William C. Kashatus, "Sparking a Rock 'n' Roll Revolution: An Interview with Dick Clark," *Pennsylvania Heritage* (Summer 1998): 15.

9. See Joseph S. Clark Jr., and Dennis Clark, "Rally and Relapse, 1946–1968," in *Philadelphia: A 300-Year History,* edited by Russel F. Weigley. (New York: W.W. Norton, 19882), 680–82.

10. Fred Bronson and Dick Clark, *Dick Clark's American Bandstand.* (New York: HarperCollins, 1997).

11. For popular histories of the 1950s and 1960s see: William Manchester, *The Glory and the Dream: A Narrative History of America, 1932–1972.* (New York: Bantam, 1974; and Mary Beth Norton, editor. *A People and a Nation: A History of the United States.* (Boston: Houghton Mifflin, 1990). For works on the history of music see: Barbara Tischler, *An American Music: The Search for an American Musical Identity.*

(New York: Oxford University, 1986); and Ronald L. Davis, *A History of Music in American Life.* (Malabar, FL: Krieger, 1982).

12. Clark & Bronson, *Dick Clark's American Bandstand,* 160.

13. Rubrics are a form of assessment that provide explicit criteria for evaluation. Designed in chart form, a rubric details the criteria for what constitutes "unsatisfactory," "satisfactory," "good," and "exceptional" student work. Rubrics are most often used along with portfolios and student self-evaluations to gain a more accurate understanding of a student's real abilities. Grant Wiggins, president and director of the Center on Learning, Assessment, and School Structure (CLASS) in Geneseo, New York, offers the most comprehensive examination of this method of assessment in *Assessing Student Performance: Exploring the Purpose and Limits of Testing.* (San Francisco: Jossey-Bass Publishers, 1993).

14. This student's work inspired me to revise my own doctoral dissertation on the Friends Public School, completed two years earlier, and publish it, in a more readable fashion, for the general public. See William C. Kashatus, *A Virtuous Education: William Penn's Vision for Philadelphia Schools.* (Wallingford, PA: Pendle Hill, 1997).

15. For more information on how to subscribe to or publish with *The Concord Review,* contact Will Fitzhugh, editor at 730 Boston Post Road, Suite 24, Sudbury, MA 01776. Phone: 800-331-5007. Website: *http://www.tcr.org*

16. See Justin Pertschuk, "The Friends Public School: A Quaker Institution in War," *The Concord Review* (Fall 1994): 47–58.

Part Three: Personal History
Teaching Methods That Inspire Other Genres
of Historical Writing

On many summer afternoons during my childhood, my grandfather and I would visit the cemetery where our family members are buried. As we made our way from gravesite to gravesite, stopping to plant flowers and trim the grass around the headstones, my grandfather shared many fascinating anecdotes about our ancestors. He spoke of the challenges faced by his immigrant parents in their struggle to assimilate into American society; about the untimely death of a younger brother in the anthracite coal mines of northeastern Pennsylvania's Wyoming Valley; and about the dreams and aspirations they had for their posterity.

My grandfather had a special talent for transforming a cemetery into a place for the living; an open classroom for family history and a forum for moral education based on an intimate legacy handed down by previous generations. He inspired me by making a personal connection to the distant, seemingly irrelevant history I learned in school.

Years later, in my effort to make that same connection for my own students, I researched, wrote, and performed annually a living history play about my great-grandfather, Peter Kashatus, who immigrated to the United States in the late nineteenth century from Vilna, Lithuania. (See Figure 3–1.) It was a gift to my grandfather for inspiring a love of history in me.

Some might say that Peter Kashatus had a rather unremarkable life. Settling in Pennsylvania's anthracite region, this son of a Lithuanian farmer made his livelihood as a coal miner. He married, raised a family of four children, and scrimped and saved so his children could go to school and make something of themselves. He looked forward to payday when he would spend some of his meager earnings at the local tavern, where alcohol was the poor man's

Figure 3–1. *The author portrays his great-grandfather, Peter Kashatus, in a one-person living history performance on an eastern European immigrant who searched for his American Dream in northeastern Pennsylvania's anthracite coal mines.*
(Photograph: Joel Zarska)

aphrodisiac. On Sundays and holy days he, like most of the parishioners, gave his time and another portion of his meager earnings to the Catholic Church. He lost a son to a mining accident and, ultimately, his own life to black lung disease. At the same time, his life's story is intimately woven into the fabric of America's Industrial Era and provides a useful context through which students can learn about the human response to immigration, assimilation, unionization, and the robber barons of the late nineteenth and early twentieth centuries. In order to make myself more convincing to the students, I use the trunk my great-grandfather brought with him through Ellis Island, his coal miner's helmet and lantern, the first American flag he owned, and photographs of his children.

Because many of my students can trace their own ancestry to the so-called "New Immigration" that came to the United States from southern and eastern Europe after the Civil War, they often find that their parents have similar anecdotes about their ancestors or similar heirlooms that have been passed down to them. These are humble reminders of immigrant families who came to the United States in search of the American Dream and its promise of a more prosperous lifestyle for their descendants.

What I want my students to understand and, eventually, to write about, is that they, too, have a personal relationship with history; that they are part of a much larger legacy handed down to them from generations of others who came before them. That legacy is informed by certain values, aspirations, and behaviors that shape who they are and, in many cases, the professions they will choose for themselves as well as the moral code by which they will raise their own children. In other words, I want them to make their own connection to the past; not to see history as distant, or irrelevant to themselves and their futures.

There are many ways to make such a personal connection to the past, especially since many of today's students are recent immigrants who can trace their family's United States citizenship back just a generation or two. The memories are more vivid, the documentation more recent. Regardless of the date of arrival in this country, many families make photograph albums, keep diaries, or plan family gatherings. Others collect family heirlooms, perform living history, or visit sites such as Ellis Island or Civil War battlefields where their ancestors made their own impact on history, however briefly. All of these methods allow people to make a more personal connection to the past than the scholarly histories, textbooks, or even made-for-TV documentaries can provide.

Of course, many academic historians tend to question these practices as legitimate historical research. They argue that unless there is a firm understanding of the historical framework, or national events that have shaped our collective past, public history is little more than a hobby. Not so, argue Roy Rosenzweig and David Thelen, authors of the recent book, *The Presence of the Past: The Meaning of History in American Life*. Rozenzweig and Thelen conducted a survey of more than 1,500 Americans of different ethnic and racial backgrounds. Interviewees were asked to respond to a series of questions about their connections to the past and encouraged to provide open-ended descriptions of their experiences with history. For most of these people, the intimate past or family history mattered most. They preferred to learn about history through museums, artifacts, and firsthand accounts because they are more personal. They used history, in this sense, to define themselves, their place in their larger family, and their family's place in the broader context of national history.

According to the authors, "approaching artifacts and sites on their own terms" allow visitors to "cut through all the intervening stories, step around the agendas that have been advanced by history professionals in the meantime, and feel as if they were experiencing a moment from the past, almost as it had originally been experienced."[1]

I share their concern. What students need is a balanced approach to history that will allow for *both* the personal and national to be integrated into the study of the past and to link the past and the present together in an active and ongoing dialogue. Why should the American Revolution interest any youngster, unless he or she can make a personal connection with it? Their ancestors need not to have fought in the War for American Independence either. A creative teacher can make a meaningful connection to the American Revolution for a student whose family immigrated to the United States from Russia during the Bolshevik Revolution, Nazi Germany, or even Castro's Cuba. The common denominator in all of these movements was a fervent desire for political and/or religious freedom. To be sure, the particular circumstances in each event differed, but not individuals' motivation to create a better life for themselves and their posterity. How that story played out in America is a very personal and moving legacy for many families, and one they are very willing to share with their children if the interest can be sparked by an encouraging teacher. Unless teachers are willing to make that kind of effort, history will, for the majority of students, become meaningless. They will have no interest in learning about a past that will be easily forgotten. And with no past, there is no hope for a better future.

Encouraging students to make a personal connection with history is the subject of Part Three. In this section I will explore a variety of methods—living history, oral history, simulations, and service learning—to inspire student interest and writing on their own relationship with the past. In writing their personal histories students learn how to apply many of the research and writing skills already discussed in earlier sections of the book, and that doing history can be fun.

Living History

Living history has, over the last decade, become one of the most popular educational and entertaining movements in our country. The National Park Service, Civil War reenactors, and individual educator-historians use living history to challenge their audiences to think and feel in ways that makes the

Figure 3–2. *The author, dressed as a Continental Army soldier, holds class in front of Washington's headquarters at Valley Forge National Historical Park.* (*Photograph: Ann Kessler*)

past come alive. Unlike traditional academic history, the practitioners of living history believe that the past can be inspirational as well as factual and that engaging the empathy of others is every bit as important as understanding history. This does not mean that accuracy is compromised for entertainment. Instead the challenge for a reenactor is to understand and present the people and events of the past as honestly and as accurately as possible. This involves integrating into the performance their words and their experiences, taken from letters, diaries, journals, or speeches. In this way, the reenactor can become part of another generation for the audience while recognizing that to do so completely is impossible. This is a matter of respecting the historical integrity of the subject itself.[2]

I have used living history in my class (see Figure 3–2) as a means of engaging students through one-man performances of such characters as: William Penn, the Quaker founder of Pennsylvania; Thomas Paine, the gadfly of the

American Revolution who wrote *Common Sense;* Thomas **Garrett**, a station master on the Underground Railroad; Virgil Caine, a small-southern-farmer-turned-Confederate soldier; Eddie Collins, a Hall of Fame baseball player; and, of course, my great-grandfather, Peter Kashatus. Each performance is followed by an open discussion of the character and his place in the larger context of American history. Students are quick to follow the lead. Many ask to do their own living history presentations. One of the most convenient ways to honor the request is through the Family History Project, a three-week assignment that encourages students to explore their family ancestries.

The assignment is given shortly before spring break so students can take the time to meet with grandparents and extended family to learn more about their ancestry. Since the vacation period often coincides with the Easter and Passover holidays, family reunions are almost always assured. Students are required to complete a family tree of at least three generations and some kind of written work. The writing can come in the form of a personal reflection piece, or a living history performance of a particular ancestor who inspired the student. For those who choose to write a one-person living history play about an ancestor, the following instructions are given:

Step 1: Researching your ancestor

1. Talk to family members, especially those who knew the subject. Find out as much as you can about the subject, including family anecdotes, personal idiosyncrasies, writings (i.e, letters, diary, memoirs) of that person.

2. Gather family heirlooms. They don't necessarily have to belong to the ancestor, but should apply to their story. Only collect those heirlooms that can be used in a play; nothing that is fragile, delicate because of age, or too valuable to share with others.

3. Establish the historical context. What time period do you want to focus on? Consider the time period in which your ancestor lived. What were the important social, political, economic, and/or cultural movements? You may want to focus on only one of these topics. Let the degree of information you can find establish the time period. Then use the text to find out more about it.

Step 2: Writing the play

1. Establish a cause-and-effect story. The play has to hold audience interest and explain why the subject took a certain course of action. This allows you, the actor, to develop your ancestor's story, as you understand it.

2. Integrate family anecdotes. Remember that "stories" whether actual, embellished, or invented always capture audience interest.

3. Find a role model at the video store. Use movies and a particular actor to give you a better idea of how you might want to portray your ancestor. This may include the accent you use, idiosyncratic behaviors, or a decision-making process.

4. Remember: All history is interpretation. Living history is no different. You are giving your interpretation of your ancestor's life.

Step 3: Performing the play

1. Gauge the play to run no more than 15 minutes. You will most likely go over.

2. Exploit one or two of the characteristics or idiosyncrasies of your ancestor throughout the play.

3. Don't get caught up in the script. Yes, you will have to commit to memory some of that script. But let your feeling of your ancestor and her or his emotions carry the play.

4. Rehearse, rehearse, rehearse—and do it in front of a mirror before you try it in front of a live audience.

The following script was completed as an assignment for the Family History Project. It offers a good example of the kind of balance I want my students to discover between their own past and national history. The play is about a student's great-grandmother who immigrated to the United States from Ireland at the turn of the nineteenth century.

STUDENT LIVING HISTORY PLAY: "NANA BATES"

(Use Irish accent and sit in chair, dressed in an old shawl and bonnet): My name is Nora Jennings and I was born on October 31, 1887, at Logboy, Bellhaunir, Mayo Ireland. Because there was no opportunity for me in that country, I immigrated to the United States in 1904 at the age of seventeen. I settled, first, in Boston with my Aunt and Uncle, Pat and Mag Cruise, who had already come over from Ireland, but eventually found employment as a domestic servant for a Yankee family in Salem, Massachusetts, named the Nasons. I was treated much better than other Irish girls who took similar jobs at that time. The Nasons treated me like one of their own.

(Speak as if reminiscing and with great pride in husband): While I was living in Salem, I met George Bates, a handsome man who worked as an iron molder. We were married on October 31, 1911. George was an ambitious man.

Like many immigrants he did not have much of a formal education. He was only able to attend public school through the grammar school level. But he was a hard worker and a likeable person in the community. I could see that he had a future in politics.

George was a Republican. In 1918 George was elected to the Massachusetts State House of Representatives, where he taught himself the business of finances. He became so good that he was considered by others to be an expert on municipal finances. In 1924 George left the state legislature to become mayor of Salem. He held that office until 1937 when he ran for and won a seat in the United States Congress. Of course, we had to leave Salem and move to Washington, D.C., where we bought a house on Buffum Street.

During our years there, George, who chaired the congressional committee that oversaw the government of Washington, became known as the "Mayor of Washington." He mixed with the common man as well as the more important people on Capitol Hill. In fact, George became a close personal friend of Senator Henry Cabot Lodge. Both of us treated everyone the same, no matter how wealthy or humble they were. We were raised to do that and we raised our children that way as well.

(Show photos of children and talk with great pride about them): Together George and I raised eight children. We provided each one with a good education and raised them to become good citizens. George was very proud of them all, especially of the five who served our country in World War II. *(Sadly):* Alas, George was not destined to see his old age. He was killed in an airplane accident at the Washington National Airport on November 1, 1949. Our eldest son, Bill, finished out his term in Congress.

(Regain composure and end on a cheerful note): As for myself, I continued to live in our house on Buffum Street. Like George, I welcomed everyone who stopped to visit, no matter what their station was in life. I was as comfortable with the elite of Washington as I was sitting on the stoop of our house and chatting with my neighbors. I passed away in 1983 with no regrets, just thankful for the wonderful blessings of family and friends I had known over the 93 years of my life.

The script reflects a nice interchange between family history and major events in our national history, including immigration, assimilation, and World War II. The student weaves these larger national movements into the dialogue as benchmarks in her ancestor's life. She discusses the proud nature of this Irish-American family who worked their way up from blue collar beginnings into the highest social circles of the nation's capitol. At the same time, they did not forget their humble beginnings, or as Nora Bates exclaims, "to treat everyone the same," no matter what their station in life was.

The student also portrayed the legacy that her ancestors bestowed on their children. That legacy was informed by humility and a lack of pretense towards other people, and also a sense of duty to country. That legacy inspired Nora's children to serve in the military during World War II, and for one to complete his father's term in Congress. Naturally there are areas that might have been better developed. Why, for example, was there no opportunity for Nora to remain in Ireland? What were the political and economic circumstances forcing her to immigrate? What factors led to George's close friendship with Senator Henry Cabot Lodge? While these issues are important to know in order to get a more complete picture of Nora Bates, the student was limited by the information at her disposal. She wasn't able to find those answers herself and where she could speculate on other issues, she leaned on the text for help. For example, the student, in relating her great-grandmother's experience as a domestic servant commented on the unusually kind treatment of her employers, compared to the more common and less tolerant attitude of affluent families who employed the so-called "Shanty Irish." A more human element was given to the performance with the student's use of family heirlooms such as the shawl and bonnet of her great-grandmother as well as family photographs and the use of an Irish accent. She perfected the accent by studying Nicole Kidman in the movie "Far and Away," about a young affluent Irish heiress who goes to America accompanied by the son of a poor Irish farmer (played by Tom Cruise) in search of adventure.

Because not all students may enjoy the information this particular individual had at her disposal, other students may have to improvise. I was particularly impressed by two other living history performances of this nature. One student did a performance of his grandfather, a hard-working plumber, who managed to save enough money to put his two sons through college. The grandfather was also a doting husband and a devout member of the Catholic Church. All things considered, he led a rather unremarkable life. But the student piqued his classmates' interest by performing a "dialogue" between his grandfather and St. Peter at the gates of heaven. Assuming the role of his grandfather, the student answered St. Peter's questions by "repeating" them aloud for the class and answering the questions in order to explain why his grandfather's life warranted admission to heaven. Since the student had no family heirlooms, he used a workman's belt, holding various tools, and dressed in workmen's clothing. Nor were there any famous characters or well-known events in the story. Instead the student relied on his own storytelling to carry the class' interest and made sure to refer to the Great Depression, World War II, and the Korean War to explain the benchmarks in his grandfather's life.

Another student performed as herself! She represented herself as a trunk that contained many items, each of which represented an important member of her family. Narrating the performance as herself, the student took a ball of yarn and knitting needle and explained how those items reminded her of her grandmother who was devoted to her family and always made clothing for her grandchildren every birthday and Christmas. The grandmother was raised during the Depression when people couldn't afford to purchase gifts so homemade presents were given instead. Next she took a yarmulke, or a man's skullcap, and explained how this represented her grandfather, a rabbi, whose parents fled Nazi Germany during the Holocaust. His faith was so important to him that he dedicated his life to the synagogue. Next the student took a stethoscope that she borrowed from her father, a physician. She talked about his love for medicine as well as the pressure he felt from his parents to become a doctor; it was their "American dream" for him. Finally, she took a pen and a notebook and explained how they represent her mother, a writer of children's stories and historical fiction. As she finished explaining each item she carefully placed it in a large trunk. Afterwards, she closed the lid and said, "This trunk represents me and the legacy of my family." Finally, she ended the performance by explaining how each of those four family members cultivated a specific interest in her and what she planned to do with her own life because of it. The only object that actually belonged to a relative was the stethoscope, all the others were contemporary items. There was no dramatic performance, rather a personal story that integrated historical events such as the Depression, the Holocaust, and the American Dream.

Not all of students' work for the Family History Project was done in the form of a living history presentation. Other students wrote personal reflections of their ancestors, narratives, or some combination of both. Regardless of their choice, all of the students had an experience with oral history, having to interview, record, and write about the reminisces of their relatives.

Oral History

Oral history, or the recording of eyewitness accounts of the past, is another valuable method of making a personal connection with history. It is an indispensable method for researching one's family history and many students also use oral history interviews to research local history paper topics that dealt with the twentieth century as well. But the value of oral history is only as good as the questions that are asked of the interviewee. Students must carefully plan the interview by reviewing whatever materials they have already gathered on their topic, then determine what kinds of questions still need to be answered. Preparing a draft outline of those questions to use during the interview itself is essential to the success of the enterprise. Sometimes an interview simply confirms many of the things the student already knows. But hopefully, it will expand students' knowledge of the subject in ways they might not have anticipated. This is especially true for those students completing research for the local history paper.

Unlike interviews for the Family History Project, students who do oral history for the research paper must often locate individuals who have firsthand knowledge about their topic. While family members, neighbors, or friends may meet certain needs, the teacher and staff at the local historical society will, most likely, be able to identify some other possibilities. Church organizations, senior citizens clubs, and retirement villages, for example, are very receptive to helping out with oral history projects.

After students identify potential interviewees, they should phone them—or better, write them—to make the request and schedule a time. A midmorning interview is best for elderly people because fatigue usually sets in afterwards. The interviewee's home is the best place to conduct the interview since the elderly are most comfortable in familiar surroundings. Students should introduce themselves in the letter and mention the name of the school. They will also want to identify the purpose for the interview and the kinds of questions they hope to ask.

In preparing for the interview, the student should practice by doing a trial with a classmate or two. Choose a topic of current interest at the school, draft a list of questions, and then do the interview. While one classmate is being interviewed, let the third observe the process and make suggestions on how to improve the technique.

Naturally, students will want to tape the actual interview for their own benefit. When tape recording be sure to: (1) ask the interviewee for his or her permission; (2) use the best tapes available; (3) leave enough blank space at the beginning of the tape to make a formal introduction later; (4) turn the tape recorder on immediately; after exchanging opening remarks, stop the tape recorder and check for sound quality; (5) don't switch the tape recorder on and off—it's better to waste some tape than to irritate the interviewee or have a broken train of thought; and (6) keep an eye on the tape so you can be sure of when to turn it over.

Here are some other things to keep in mind:

- Be polite and courteous at all times, paying careful attention to the narrator's responses.
- Let the narrator tell her or his story. Limit your own remarks to questioning and clarification.
- Ask questions that require more than a simple "yes" or "no" response. Start the question with "How," "Where," or "What kind of . . ."
- Ask one question at a time and try to make it brief. Don't "overload" the narrator.

- Begin your interview with noncontroversial questions. After becoming better acquainted, then address the more sensitive issues. Be conscious of the narrator's body language and response. You do not want to insult or alienate your interviewee.

- Silence is common in an interview. Don't let it scare you. Use silent time to jot down a note or two.

- Be careful not to interrupt a story. Although you may not think the information is relevant to your needs at the time of the interview, it may turn out to be some of the most helpful information you receive. If the narrator strays too far from the topic, try to draw the interviewee back with a simple request such as: "Before we move on, I'd like to find out . . . "

- Do not challenge accounts that you may think are inaccurate. You can do that on paper afterward. Simply ask for clarification if you identify a discrepancy in the narrator's account.

- Always try to establish a context during the interview. You need to know what role the interviewee played in the event being described in order to understand whether the information is hearsay or an eyewitness account.

- Do not conduct an interview much past an hour in length, lest you wear out your welcome.

Finally, an oral interview follows the same protocol as written research. Students must obtain permission from the interviewees to use the information on the tape. Later, this information will have to be included in the bibliography and citations for the research paper. Students should take along a release form when they go to the interview, explain its purpose, and have the interviewee sign it. The permission form makes the process more credible. Below is a suggested release form:

I, (Interviewee's name) hereby grant permission to be tape recorded and interviewed by (name of student and name of school). I understand that this tape recording will be used for educational purposes and any publication of it, or parts of it, will be used only in a scholarly work. I do not expect, nor will I accept, any remuneration for this interview or its subsequent publication.

_____   _____
(Name of Interviewee)   *(Name of Interviewer)*

_____   _____
(Address of Interviewee)   *(Date of Interview)*

Some of the very best student research is completed through oral history interviews, especially in the Family History Project. The following essay is an example of one student's integration of personal reflection and good, solid oral history research. The essay is the product of several interviews, including those of his parents, and members of the extended family.

"REFLECTIONS OF BENJAMIN SMALL AND THE BEGINNINGS OF THE MOVIE INDUSTRY"

My childhood memories will always include visits to my grandparents' home in Hempstead, New York, a Long Island suburb of New York City. Visits usually centered around multiple trips to the movies—not the "stand-in-line-for-the-latest-Disney-release" variety of movie trips—but the "walk-right-past-the-lines-cost-free" variety of movie trips.

My grandfather seemed to know every theater manager on Long Island, and by uttering three magic words—"small film delivery"—the doors of all theaters were opened for me. Until just recently, I never realized that those three, small words were not only synonymous with a free movie pass, but a wonderful account of the American Dream and how that dream came to fruition for my great-grandfather, Benjamin Small.

Benjamin, whose name was actually "Shmuel," was the youngest son of Batsheva and Zelik Smolnick, who fled a pogrom in Riga, Latvia, in 1887. Shmuel, his parents, and his brothers and sisters made their way to Palestine and were among the first settlers to attempt to farm the inhospitable swampland of Hadera. For the next fifteen years the Smolnick family tried to eke a living out of the land, but their efforts (along with malaria) claimed the lives of all of Shmuel's older siblings. In 1902, Batsheva, pregnant again, took her surviving son to the United States and left the seventeen-year-old with a cousin in New York. She then returned to Palestine to give birth to her last child, a son named Abraham.

Shmuel, renamed "Benjamin," spoke no English, had but a few dollars in his pocket, and knew only his cousin Jacob in a city that was rapidly becoming a world metropolis. My great-grandfather was one of a steady flood of immigrants who provided a huge pool of cheap labor to fuel small manufacturing businesses. He lived on the Lower East Side in a crowded tenement, as did most Eastern European Jewish immigrants. Unlike the other unskilled immigrants, though, Benjamin had learned the skill of bookbinding from his father, and found employment at Doubleday and Company.

Little has been passed on about his early years in the United States. I know that he married my great-grandmother, Henrietta Maurer, in 1910, and that two years later, in 1912, they moved to Hempstead on Long Island, not far from Doubleday's new facility at Garden City, New York. There, they began their own family.

Long Island was little more than farm land in those days, but as the population of Manhattan exploded more New Yorkers came to settle there, following the newly built train lines eastward. Soon, Hempstead became the commercial hub and the largest of three existing towns on Long Island. Many of the merchants were Jewish immigrants who, like Benjamin, followed the train lines eastward. Together these displaced Jews formed a congregation, Beth

Israel, where they were free to practice their religion without fear of the government-sanctioned reprisals they had experienced in Europe.

Before the outbreak of World War I, my great-grandfather purchased a car and moonlighted as a taxi driver, ferrying soldiers to and from the train station and Camp Mills Army Base, five miles outside of Hempstead. Having been exempted from service, he continued his work at Doubleday into the early 1920s.

One stormy winter night in 1921, a blizzard put the Long Island Railroad out of commission, presenting a major problem for the manager of Hempstead's only movie theater. Without the railroad from New York City, he could not secure the reels of nitrate film he needed to run the movie theater. The manager hired Benjamin to drive through the blizzard and into New York to pick up the film and deliver it to him in Hempstead. The rest is film delivery history.

During the 1920s motion picture production, distribution, and exhibition became a major industry and the movies and their stars became a national obsession. Theaters proliferated, and Benjamin, who had earned a reputation for delivering film on time despite inclement weather, found it necessary to purchase trucks to run his film delivery business. While other industries suffered during the Depression, the movies provided an inexpensive escape for the masses. My great-grandfather's financial success allowed him to purchase several properties in Hempstead, and to make a significant contribution to the construction of a beautiful new synagogue that would house the growing Beth Israel congregation.

Like most Jewish immigrants, Benjamin placed a great value on education. Despite his own lack of formal education (or perhaps because if it), both of his sons studied to become professionals; one a physician, and the other, my grandfather, an accountant. My grandfather received his degree from the Wharton School at the University of Pennsylvania. By that time, however, Benjamin and Henrietta were in poor health and my grandfather and his brother returned to Hempstead to run the family business. Henrietta died in 1953, and Benjamin shortly after.

Benjamin Small found the United States to be a "goldene medina" (Yiddish for "golden country"). His American Dream was realized in less than a generation and his sons enjoyed a financial security not known to many. The importance he placed on education continues to live on as the proceeds from his small film delivery business have sent my mother to college, helped my father through law school, and have established trust accounts for each of his seventeen great-grandchildren.

Just as important to him was his Jewish faith. Benjamin maintained contact with his younger brother, Abe, in Israel, helping to support him and the Zionist effort to create a permanent Jewish homeland in Palestine. Although Benjamin considered himself to be an American, he, like other American Jews, identified very closely with the land that claimed the lives of his older siblings, Israel. In fact, my grandfather was bar mitzvahed in Palestine, no small feat in 1938.

Today when I visit my grandparents in the home that my great-grandfather built for them half a century ago, I find a Hempstead that is well past its prime. The synagogue that was Benjamin's pride and joy still stands, but, unable to be supported by a dwindling Jewish population, it has been a Korean church for the past twenty years. Congregation Beth Israel continues to meet in a converted house. The end of the train line is now Montauk, one hundred miles to the east, where, coincidentally, there is a movie theater. In fact, there are more than two hundred movie theaters on Long Island that are serviced by Small Film Delivery and will continue to depend on this service until technology can transmit movies digitally.

My grandfather, now 73 years old, and my Uncle David have been known to "rescue" cases of film during the worst blizzards, or to "do the Montauk run" at 3:00 a.m. when a driver is sick. My great-grandfather Benjamin Small would be proud to know that through three generations the show has always gone on!

Like the earlier living history play, this essay places family history within a national context. Themes such as immigration, suburbanization, and the development of the movie industry are intimately related to Benjamin Small's search for the American Dream. Those themes play out in the framework of a Jewish immigrant family, which enhances the learning process for the other students in the class. During this student's presentation his classmates not only got an appreciation for a social group different from their own, but a basis with which to compare their family's history. What also impressed me about this essay was the student's own insights on the values that shaped his great-grandfather's legacy—education, Judaism, and family—and how that legacy influenced the lives of his parents and even his own life through the establishment of educational trust funds.

Living history and oral history projects are only two methods a teacher can use to make the learning process more enjoyable for students. Simulation exercises are also an exciting way for students to develop the critical reading, writing, and thinking skills that are essential to good history instruction.

Simulation Exercises

Students love role-playing, especially simulation games in which each student is assigned a specific role and must adhere to a particular set of interests of that role in a given situation. One of the most popular exercises I've used is recreating the Federal Convention of 1787 and assigning each student the role of a particular delegate.[3] There are three objectives to the exercise: (1) to give the student a better understanding of the interests, motives, and dilemmas of the framers who took part in the Constitutional Convention than they might otherwise achieve by reading about it; (2) to encourage the critical thinking skills necessary to form an argument and defend that argument in a public forum; and (3) to work within a group dynamic, cooperatively, to reach agreement on a solution that will meet the needs and interests of the largest number of delegates. In this case, the "solution" is the drafting of a constitution.

Each student is assigned one of the following delegates. Depending on class size, two or more students may be assigned one delegate and collectively they form a delegation. Each delegate (or delegation) is responsible for defending that particular delegate's constellation of interests during the convention. Among the original delegates were:

- Gunning Bedford, Jr.: small state; southern state; favors strong national government; wealth is landed, or based on property-holdings.
- Roger Sherman: small state; northern state; favors strong national government; wealth is liquid, or based on trade and commerce.
- William Few: small, southern state; strong gov't.; liquid.
- John Langdon: small, northern state; strong gov't.; landed.
- Abraham Baldwin: small, southern state; weak gov't.; liquid.
- Jonathan Dayton: small, northern state; weak gov't.; landed.
- Luther Martin: small, southern state; weak gov't.; landed.
- William Livingston: small, northern state; weak gov't.; liquid.
- George Mason: large, southern state; strong gov't.; landed.
- Robert Morris: large, northern state; strong gov't.; liquid.
- George Wythe: large, southern state; strong gov't.; liquid.
- James Wilson: large, northern state; strong gov't.; landed.
- John Blair: large, southern state; weak gov't.; liquid.
- John Lansing: large, northern state; weak gov't.; landed.
- William Davie: large, southern state; weak gov't.; landed.
- Robert Yates: large, northern state; weak gov't.; liquid.

Some of the better-known delegates are purposefully omitted, such as Benjamin Franklin, Alexander Hamilton, James Madison, and George Washington. To add Franklin, Hamilton, or Madison, whose activities are well-known to students, would limit student initiative to find out more about the delegate they are representing. The role of Washington, who served as the president of the convention, of course, is reserved for the teacher.

Students are encouraged to research their delegate to learn more about them as well as where they would be willing to compromise. This doesn't mean that they have to remain true to their delegate's lead, especially if it will prevent compromising with another delegate whose proposal seems especially attractive.[4] Students are also given a list of all delegates and their interests so they know who they might approach during the convention. As they sound out the other delegates, students find areas of mutual agreement and compromise. The more the delegates know about the interests and attitudes of each other, the better their bargaining position becomes.

Students also become familiar with the agenda of the convention before it begins. These are the issues they will debate and eventually vote on:

Legislative Branch: (1) Number of houses: one, two; (2) members chosen by: people, state legislature, state or federal executive; (3) representation: by state (equal), number of people (proportional); (4) term of office: one, two, three, four, six, more years.

Powers of the Legislature: (1) taxation: yes, no; import, export; (2) commerce: yes, no; interstate commerce only, intra-state; (3) military: declare war, raise an army, navy, call out the state's militias; (4) slavery: regulate or not.

Powers Denied the States: (1) make treaties: yes, no; (2) coin money: yes, no; (3) impair obligations of contracts: yes, no; (4) export, import duties: yes, no.

Executive: (1) number: one or more; (2) election: people directly, state legislatures, federal legislature, other; (3) term: one, two, three, four, five, six, more years.

Powers of the Executive: (1) military: declare war, commander-in-chief; (2) treaty-making: alone, with legislature, submit to people, submit to legislature; (3) impeachment: legislature, people, courts; simple majority, or two-thirds.

Courts: (1) selection by: executive, legislature, people; (2) judicial review of legislative and executive acts: yes, no; (3) length of term: one, two, three, four, five, six, more years.

Ratification of Constitution: (1) who, people, states; (2) how: simple majority, two-thirds, unanimous.

Generally, the convention takes place over a six- to eight-day period of time, depending on class time. For example, those schools using block scheduling with periods that are 90 minutes or longer will only need six sessions. With 45- or 50-minute periods, the convention will take all eight days. The first day is spent orienting students to the convention, the agenda, its rules, and the various delegates. Days 2 through 6 are spent making proposals before the full convention, answering questions of clarification, debating, and, ultimately, voting on proposals. Most of the lobbying—securing the appropriate number of signatures on a proposal, and persuading other delegates to support a proposal before the vote actually takes place—occurs outside of the classroom. One class session can be scheduled for this purpose in order to familiarize students with the process.

I usually divide the convention into five days: day 1 addresses the legislative branch and its powers; day 2, the powers denied the states; day 3, the executive branch and its powers; day 4, the courts; and day 5, the ratification of the constitution. During each of these days the delegates are required to observe the following rules:

1. Each delegation, represented by one or more students, has only one vote during each ballot taken at the convention. If there is more than one student in a delegation, majority rule decides. If a delegation of two members, for example, cannot reach agreement, the delegation loses its vote.

2. All proposals must be written out on the following proposal form and signed by three other delegates (delegations). If a delegation wishes to bring a different proposal to the attention of the convention, the proposal must also be written out on another proposal form and signed.

PROPOSAL

Delegation Name: _____
Issue pertaining to constitution: _____
We hereby respectfully submit the following proposal to this Convention:
It is proposed that: _____
_____
_____
The purpose in making this proposal is to: _____
_____
Signature: _____
Consenting delegates (delegations): _____
_____
_____

3. For a proposal to become part of the working draft of the convention, it must receive a majority of all votes cast.

4. If any delegate wishes to introduce a proposal or to speak for or against them, he or she must ask the chair for recognition. George Washington, as convention chairman, has the sole right to recognize delegates. He must determine fairly the order in which delegates (delegations) should speak.

5. Certain rules of procedure will be decided upon by the delegates and the chairman, such as the number of speeches allowed, pro and con, for any proposal made, and how long those speeches may be.

6. Delegates are required to keep a journal, writing a report of their activities in the convention on a daily basis. This daily report must include: votes cast, efforts to gain support, and compromises made. These reports must be turned into the teacher each day.

As previously mentioned, writing takes place in the form of a daily journal which I collect and review on a daily basis. Each entry describes, in the first person, the activities of that particular delegate at a given day's session. Not only must the students describe their activities, but they must also explain why they took a particular action in the context of their specific constellation of interests. The final entry must address the students' views on the convention itself and how successful they felt it was. The following entries were completed by a student who represented Luther Martin, who was the Attorney General of Maryland. Hailing from a small, southern state, he was a bellicose defender of states' rights. But as the Convention evolved, he softened his position and agreed to serve on the Connecticut Compromise Committee, which advocated a bicameral legislature with one house based on equal representation and the other on proportional representation. Of course, this so-called "Great Compromise" was adopted by the convention and laid the structural foundations of the current national legislature.

JOURNALS OF THE FEDERAL CONVENTION—
LUTHER MARTIN

Session One: The first day of the convention was a lot different than what I expected. I was definitely not as prepared as I should have been to debate and defend my proposal. I had not thought through the issues pertaining to the legislative branch very well because I wasn't aware of the flexibility I had in writing the proposal. My intention was to propose a weak central government. But the way I interpreted a "weak" government was to have a two-house legislature with each house having a check over the other. I wanted this legislature chosen by the people because I fear that a strong national government will deny the people their basic rights. If a larger number of people have the right to elect the legislature, then there is a better chance that the legislature will act according to the needs of the majority. It was also important to me that representation in the legislature be equal coming from a small state.

I do not want this legislature to have the right to impose taxes; that power should be left to the states for their own needs. Nor do I want any central government regulating slavery because many people in my state depend upon slave labor to farm their land. But I do want the legislature to be able to raise an army and navy and to declare war. Since I come from a small state, our militia may not be adequately prepared to defend us if we are attacked by another country.

I didn't have much difficulty in finding support for my proposal. I was able to convince Jonathan Dayton to sign my proposal because his wealth was tied to property-holding and though, being a northerner, he disagreed with slavery on moral grounds, he saw the importance of protecting an individual's property when it was tied to slaves. I was able to convince William Few, who wanted a strong central government, that giving the legislature the power to impose taxes would threaten his own wealth because it was tied to commerce or liquid assets and he would have less control over it than if the states exercised that power.

This student has no pretense. She was willing to admit her shortcomings and concerns, which was very valuable in identifying the trouble spots in her understanding of the process. Her entries created a constructive dialogue between us and she was able to act quite effectively in the remaining four sessions of the convention because of it. In this particular entry she is concerned over her "misinterpretation" of a "weak" central government. She didn't need to be. While Martin interpreted "weak" government to mean a government that would defer to "states rights," I do not want the student to simply mimic the delegate they are representing. As long as they can explain their understanding of a "weak" central government, that is more important to me. In fact, this student's explanation and the powers she denied the national legislature (i.e., regulating slavery and power to impose taxes) were very consistent with her role as a states rights advocate as well as her insistence on a bicameral legislature based on equal representation and beholden to the people. What's more, she was an effective lobbyist to cut across regional differences with Jonathan Dayton, a northerner, and have him sign a proposal that protected the right of the states to determine matters of slavery.

The student who was assigned George Wythe offers a fine example of the exchange of views that occurs in the convention. Wythe, a college professor and lawyer, was part of the Virginia delegation that favored a strong national government with a legislature based on proportional representation. Wythe, in particular, wanted a single executive with the power to veto all legislation, to pardon, to pass treaties, and to act as commander-in-chief of the military. Unable to secure the passage of his own proposal, Wythe made a deal with James Wilson (large, northern state, who favored a strong national government). Wilson agreed to support Wythe's earlier proposal for proportional representation in the national legislature, in turn for the Virginian's support for an executive with more limited powers.

JOURNAL OF GEORGE WYTHE

Session Two: Today we heard the debates of and voted on the proposals of the executive branch and its powers. Two proposals were debated, one by James Wilson and the other by Robert Yates. I signed Wilson's proposal, but had to make some drastic compromises in order for it to pass.

Wilson proposed a one man executive elected directly by the people for a four year term. He would act as the commander-in-chief of the military and had veto power. He could only pass treaties with the advice and consent of the legislature, and he did not have the power to pardon. If for some reason he became corrupt, the executive could be impeached by both the courts and by two-thirds majority vote of the state legislatures.

By allowing the executive to be elected by the people, we gained the votes of many large state delegates. I would have liked the executive to have all of the powers possible and to have him elected by the state legislature, but I was willing to compromise on those two issues because Wilson had signed my proposal for a national legislature based on proportional representation. Besides, Wilson's proposal still provides for a more powerful executive than Yates did.

Yates wanted a four-man executive elected by the people for a three-year term. This executive cabinet could declare war and had veto power. But all of his other powers were checked by the national legislature, and all members of the cabinet could be impeached by the national legislature by a slight majority.

The primary focus of the debate between these two proposals was over the number of people the executive branch should include. While many of the small states were concerned that one man would wield too much power and wanted to have a multiple executive, most of the large state delegates understood that emergency situations, like war, demanded a single executive who can make a decision quickly if necessary instead of opening to debate among others.

Ultimately, Wilson's proposal won by a vote of eight to four in favor, with four courteous abstentions, but only after the supporters of the Wilson proposal agreed to two amendments. First, there would be a "back-up" executive who would advise the main executive and, in case of impeachment or death in office, become the chief executive. Second there will be an advisory cabinet appointed by the chief executive to offer him counsel on both foreign and domestic affairs.

Naturally the practice of keeping daily journals and responding to them is labor intensive for both the students and myself, but the dividends are great in terms of student understanding of and appreciation for the framers of our U.S. Constitution.

Day 7 is spent reviewing and amending the constitution the class has drafted during the previous five days. The final day is spent comparing that document to the actual United States Constitution that was ratified in 1789. I am always impressed by the insightful discussion that occurs during these last two days. The act of reviewing a typed copy of the class' constitution often sparks concerns about things that are conspicuously absent, such as a section that addressed the protection of individual rights against the encroaching power of the national government. There are also concerns that are age-based, such as lowering the voting age to sixteen, removing property qualifications for enfranchisement, requiring or not requiring military service, and an explicit statement on female and racial equality. One of the most interesting class constitutions I saw made sure to include all of these measures:

History Class Constitution of 1787

Article I: Legislative Branch
Section 1. All legislative powers herein granted shall be vested in a Congress of the United States that shall consist of one house.
Section 2. Representatives of this houses will be chosen by the people (i.e., all those who live in the United States age sixteen and above, regardless of race, sex, creed or property qualifications) and serve a three year term.
Section 3. Representation in this house will be based on the proportion of people in each state.
Section 4. The Congress shall have the power to make all legislation, approve all executive appointments and treaties by two-thirds majority vote, and to determine war, to raise an army and navy.

Article II: Powers given the States
Section 1. Full faith and credit shall be given in each state to lay and collect taxes on all national and international imports and exports. One-third of all tax monies must be turned over to the national government to be spent for the general welfare of all the people in the United States.

Article III: Executive Branch
Section 1. The executive branch shall be vested in a President of the United States of America and an alternate and a cabinet of advisors in order to enforce the laws of the land. The President, his alternate, and his cabinet shall hold their offices for a term of four years and be elected by the people (as defined above) directly.
Section 2. The President shall have the power with the advice and consent of the Congress to make foreign treaties and appoint members of the judiciary. He has the power to veto legislation and the authority to set the national budget and spend that money with the approval of Congress.
Section 3. The President is Commander-in-Chief of the United States of America.
Section 4. The President can be impeached by two-thirds majority vote of Congress or the judicial branch.

Article IV: Judicial Branch
Section 1. A Supreme Court will be chosen by the people (as defined above) directly for a three-year term.
Section 2. The Supreme Court has the power to review all legislation and acts of both the legislative and executive branches to determine the constitutionality of those acts.

Article V: Ratification of the Constitution The ratification of the constitution will be completed by the states and approval will be by two-thirds majority of the states.

Bill of Rights: The national government will guarantee the protection of all of the following individual freedoms: of worship; of speech; of press; of assembly; of privacy; of innocence unless proven guilty of a crime by a jury of peers. All of these rights will be observed for all United States citizens age 16 and above, regardless of sex, race, creed or property qualifications.

By comparing their own constitution to the actual one, students gain an appreciation for the difficulty of nation building and the responsibilities of citizenship. I find that they have a stronger interest in the constitutional history we study later in the course as well as current events, particularly in Supreme Court decisions that wrestle with the framers' original intent. In this sense, there is a sense of ownership that is cultivated by the convention that goes well beyond the reading of the text and the regurgitation of information on a test or even in the writing of an essay on the subject. Since the convention takes place early in the school year, students become excited about history class. They also come to anticipate that same kind of engagement on other topics as the course unfolds.

While no other simulation exercise is as engaging as the Constitutional Convention, there are others I use in the course. "Reconstructing the Union" after the Civil War, for example, is a wonderful way for students to understand the intricacies of race relations and sectional rivalry. I will have students get the appropriate background information they need to complete this simulation by reading their text and then divide the class into five groups: Radical Republicans, who are bent on justifying the costs of war by eliminating all political rights of Confederate leaders, helping freedmen to adjust to political citizenship and equal economic opportunity, and remaking southern society in the image of the North; Northern Moderates, or Republicans and Democrats, intent on a speedy reconciliation between North and South based on leniency, amnesty, and merciful readmission of the southern states to the Union; ex-Confederates, or the old southern planter aristocracy, who want to restore traditional plantation-based market-crop economy with blacks as a cheap labor force; small, independent southern farmers, who want to displace the planter class politically and create greater economic diversity in the South; Black Freedmen, who seek physical protection from abuse by local whites, economic independence, political participation, and educational opportunity. During a five-day period, these groups debate lobby and propose solutions to the following issues:

> *Readmission of the Confederate States:* Under what conditions should they be admitted? What should the process of readmission be? Who should supervise this process?

> *Status of Black Freedmen:* What political rights should they have? How should these rights be guaranteed? By who? Should the freedmen be given any compensation for their former status as slaves? What kind?

> *Treatment of ex-Confederate officers and government officials:* Should they be readmitted? If they are readmitted, should they be given the

same privileges as the ordinary southerner? Any special compensation? Punishment?

Student writing is, like the Constitutional Convention, completed in the form of a daily journal and, afterwards, an analytical essay, still in first person, addressing the outcome of the convention and prospects for the future of the country.

I have done similar simulations on the 1848 Seneca Falls Convention on Women's Rights, Indian Removal, the post-World War I peace settlement at Versailles, and the Cuban Missile Crisis. In each case, the key to the success of the simulation depended on the degree to which students felt a sense of ownership, or being involved directly in the planning, execution, and writing exercises of each simulation.

Service Learning

Unlike "community service" programs, which stress voluntarism for the intangible reward of the experience itself, service learning can be integrated into the history curriculum by emphasizing preparation before engaging in a particular project and providing structured time for students to think, talk, or write about what they did and saw during the actual service activity. Service learning not only enhances the curriculum by extending it beyond the classroom and developing substantive knowledge and practical skills, but also cultivates a sense of social responsibility and civic-mindedness.[5] But service learning demands a sustained commitment on the part of both students and teachers as well as an innovative approach to education that focuses on learning by doing outside of the traditional classroom environment. The key to creating a successful service learning experience for students is to establish a well-organized project that stresses both preparation for and reflection of the service experience. Journal writing is one of the more meaningful ways to do this.

I use journal writing as a tool to respond to and reflect on their service experience. It is not used as a personal diary, or for free writing. Journals contain student responses to: readings I've assigned to give them a better understanding of the service project; observations and questions that arise from their service experience; and a tracking device to record the progress or lack of progress of the service project. I do not grade the journals, but rather use them to initiate a dialogue, sometimes with the individual student and at other times, with the entire class.[6]

One of my classes decided to engage in a service learning project because of a concern they had about the impact of poverty on inner-city youth. Our study of Philadelphia's history revealed that local government rarely invested the financial or human resources to improve the living conditions or educational opportunities for children of the city's poor. The class wanted to address that need in a more concrete way than writing to local representatives or petitioning City Council for change. What follows are excerpts from student journals describing the project, how it began, and the rewards and concerns of the experience.

> *Student Journal 1:* Our class has been talking about getting involved in a service project because of our concern for disadvantaged kids in the city. Dr. Kashatus has made an appointment for class members at the University of Pennsylvania to become involved in the Greater Philadelphia Partnership. Not everyone was happy about the fact that this project is going to be required for the course. Some kids think that requiring community service contradicts the spirit of helping others, which should be voluntary. I've done community service before, but this sounds different. I'm not too sure if I understand how it will help me understand American history, but if it gets me out of class time, I'll certainly try it!

This student, like so many others at Penn Charter, had done community service in the past. She realized that service involved giving one's time and, usually, labor to a volunteer organization. But the concept of learning American history, or, in this case, Philadelphia's history, by doing service was confusing. Her curiosity and desire to "get out of the classroom" allowed her to keep an open mind. There were other students who did not appreciate the fact that this was a required part of the course. Some of those would change their mind. Others begrudgingly participated throughout the project.

Since service learning was a relatively new concept, I thought it best to join an organization that had some experience with it. The University of Pennsylvania proved to be that organization. Penn coordinates the Greater Philadelphia High School Partnership, a program that is based on regional cooperation. The premise is that regional cooperation is an economic and a cultural necessity at a time when many Philadelphians live in segregated, poverty-stricken neighborhoods and those who live in the more affluent suburbs have divorced themselves from any responsibility to the city. Other cities that have merged with their suburbs have less concentrated poverty, less income disparity, less residential and school segregation, and lower crime rates.[7] It follows that if this same concept of regionalism occurred in the Philadelphia area, that the region would be safer, cleaner, and more economically viable. The Greater Philadelphia Partnership promotes the concept of regionalism by bringing together high school students from public, private, and parochial schools from both the city and suburbs in a service-based partnership. In this way, the program hopes to increase civic awareness among young people by allowing them to make a positive contribution to the Philadelphia area through service learning and to build trust and friendships among students of a different race, social class, and family income.[8] The following entry describes the initial meeting with our partner schools:

> **Student Journal 2:** Yesterday about 100 public, private, and parochial schools met at Penn to discuss the idea of regionalism and to organize service projects that will promote that idea. Penn Charter was assigned to a group that also included [an inner-city public school, a suburban parochial school, and a private boarding school in the suburbs]. I have to admit that the kids from the two suburban schools were too preppie for my taste. When we sat down to lunch it sounded to me as if all they were concerned about was using the experience on their transcript to get into a competitive college. All the kids from [the inner city public school] were black and stayed pretty much to themselves. I wonder if they were testing us to see if they would really commit to the project. When we finally sat down and talked about it, we all wanted a project that would have an immediate improvement instead of a long-term project, like tutoring elementary school students. We all decided to restore a city playground. We also decided that four committees would be set up at each school to be responsible for site identification, recruiting student volunteers, and raising money to pay for project expenses. While I don't want to sound too conceited, the Penn Charter students carried the discussion. We knew what we wanted to do and how to do it. I only hope that we didn't come off as "know-it-alls."

This student's insights were especially interesting. Like several classmates, he had already been involved with community service projects. In fact, he quickly assumed a leadership role in the discussion and suggested the playground idea that was eventually accepted by the others. His insight that the students from the two suburban schools were "using the service project to get into a competitive college" was also not that farfetched and it also serves as a motivator for many of the students at Penn Charter. Voluntarism sounds good to students, particularly in the junior year. They are aware that colleges are looking for substantive extracurricular involvements and service is one of the most attractive involvements because it suggest social awareness. While that sounds manipulative, "service-for-college-admission" is, for many, only the key that opens the door to a more altruistic commitment to service for the sake of the experience itself. After I read this and similar entries in the journals of other students, we discussed them as a class and decided that regardless of the student's particular motive, our class would keep their commitment in order to get the most out of the experience. That discussion took place in early October.

For the next two months, the Penn Charter students carried out their responsibilities in setting up the four committees and doing the required reading I assigned to better prepare them for the project. Unfortunately, the only other school to do the same was the inner-city public school. The two suburban schools dropped out, most likely because they realized just how much work would be involved. Some of my students became very discouraged. Others, who had never been keen on the idea, tried to convince their classmates to abandon the project altogether, as reflected in the following entry.

Student Journal 3: [In early December] a group [of Penn Charter students] met with the commissioner of the Philadelphia Recreation Department to select a site. We wanted either a recreation center or playground that was in an inner city area and would give 10 to 15 students enough work for two or three months. We selected Vare Recreation Center in Gray's Ferry. This was in a South Philadelphia neighborhood that was mostly populated by blacks. The city had already put a new roof on the center and Penn Charter would be responsible for scraping, painting and cleaning the gym, the hallways, and the upstairs that was used for dance classes.

We kicked off the project on Martin Luther King's birthday. When I walked into the place I was shocked. Graffiti covered most of the walls and the gym was badly in need of a new paint job. Water damage had discolored the walls and large pieces of paint were peeling away from the walls. About six kids from [the inner city public school] showed up. All the rest were from our history class. There were about 22 kids in all.

Dr. Kashatus sat us all down and told us about the history of the neighborhood. In the early 20th century, mostly poor white immigrants and blacks lived there. He explained how this area of South Philadelphia was a lot like the Seventh ward of Center City where W. E. B DuBois researched his book, *The Philadelphia Negro,* and that the crime and poverty in both of these places was not because of race, but because of racial prejudice and job competition with white immigrants. Vare was built for the children of these people. The rec allowed them to come together, to develop their bodies, and have a place where they could hang out without getting into trouble. I guess I can see that point of view. But I believe that if blacks, like whites, work hard they can get themselves out of poverty. After all, white immigrants were in the same boat. They might not have been slaves, but many of them were wage slaves when they came to this country having to work in coal mines and steel mills for next to nothing.

After, we all picked up brooms, water buckets and putty knives and got to work. We spent from 10:30 am to 4:30 pm scraping, cleaning, and sweeping, and, I think, didn't make too much of a difference. Since we're only required to go two times, I'll go for the next couple weeks when my other friends are going.

Because of the students' disillusionment, I tried to make the most out of the service project by making it a learning experience. Realizing that I would have difficulty getting all twenty students in the class to volunteer on a weekly basis, I reduced the requirement to two Saturdays over the course of the project and hoped that the experience itself would cultivate more of a commitment. At the very least, I would be able to get six to eight students a week for two months and, with some luck and a lot of hard work, we would be able to complete the painting.

Realizing that without integrating the project into my curriculum the benefits to students would be minimal, I also assigned excerpts from W. E. B. DuBois' classic study, *The Philadelphia Negro,* and Cornel West's short, provocative book, *Race Matters.*[9] While I hoped that the former would give my students an historical understanding of the roots of urban poverty and why we were undertaking this project, the latter book caused quite a heated discussion in class. Like the above student who believes "that if blacks, like whites, work hard they can get themselves out of poverty," many of my white students come from Eastern European backgrounds. Their ancestors worked as wage slaves in blue collar jobs, scrimping and saving to send the most promising of their children off to college so they could achieve a more prosperous future. These students tend to take a "color-blind" stance in discussions on race, emphasizing the importance of individual character rather than race as a determinant of social or economic class. Many of my black students have difficulty with that argument, as reflected by the following journal entry.

Student Journal 4: Today we discussed *Race Matters* in class and I had to speak up. West is absolutely correct—race DOES matter. It's difficult to put aside your differences with white people when the rest of society only seems to emphasize them. It all comes down to the "haves" and the "have-nots." For so long, blacks have been relegated to the latter category that we find greater security among our own race.

I realize that Penn Charter, as a Quaker school, tries to teach its students to be colorblind. It tries to emphasize that we all have "that of God in us" no matter what the color of our skin. But did you ever ask yourself why so few blacks actually belong to the Society of Friends?

Now we're doing this service project at Vare and all of my white class-mates think they're doing such a great service because they're helping out poor black kids. But how many of them take the time to shoot baskets with the neighborhood kids when they come in to the gym on Saturdays?

It wasn't that this student was trying to defend her black friends who were more comfortable in a separate culture, or why all the black students choose to sit together in our school's cafeteria, or even to criticize the pale complexion of the religious denomination to which I belong, as much as she was trying to explain them. In fact, she had a special gift for building bridges between black and white students by establishing an integrated gospel choir at our school and through her work in our school's growing service program. Her words inspired many of her classmates during the next few weeks of the project.

Student Journal 5: We've been working at Vare for nearly two months now and we can see the results. Most Saturdays we have ten or twelve students volunteer. It's become easier and even enjoyable to get the work done. We've given the rec center a whole new atmosphere. The bright colors and the scent of fresh paint make the hallways and upstairs seem clean. We've even painted sports figures on the walls of the gym. On one wall there's a basketball player. On another, a gymnast, and on another, a football player. We made sure to represent all races—black, white, and Hispanic—in respect for all the kids in the neighborhood.

I think the greatest reward, though, has been getting to know the neigh-borhood kids. About three weeks ago some of us started playing pick-up [basketball] with them in the gym. Others started hanging out with the girls from the neighborhood who take ballet on the second floor. For many of us, it was the first time we've ever been around inner city kids. We learned that they have many of the same interests we do. We all want the same things: a safe place to hang out, close friends, and a good education.

While I learned a lot about urbanization, racism, and humanitarian re-form in Philadelphia's history, the real benefit of this project, for me, has been the reality check it provides. I guess more than anything else, Vare allows me to be grateful for so many of the things I take for granted in my life.

Unfortunately, that entry proved to be the last one for the project. In March, a black woman, her teenage son, and her nephew were assaulted by a group of white men in the Gray's Ferry neighborhood. Shortly after, a white teenager was gunned down inside a drugstore not far from the Vare Recreation Center, allegedly by two African American men. The incident set off charges in the community that the slaying was racially motivated. In response, the Gray's

Ferry Community Action Group called for a march to protest racism. The Nation of Islam gave its full support to the march and vowed to bring in some 5,000 African American members, including Nation of Islam leader Louis Farrakhan. Despite Mayor Ed Rendell's success in lessening the possibility of a race riot by suggesting a rally to "decry racism of all kinds throughout the City of Philadelphia and the country," Penn Charter's administration believed for reasons of safety, it was best to suspend the project.[10]

If you had asked me at the outset if I could have predicted the outcome, I would have said, "no." Service learning is as unpredictable as the students who become involved in it and the events beyond our control that influence it. But that is why there are also many pleasant surprises. I began the project with the hope that the experience would cultivate social awareness in my students. For some, it did far more than that. In her final journal, one of my students wrote an entry that was later reprinted on the Commentary Page of the *Philadelphia Inquirer* under the title, "A Young Voice on Voluntarism: Could I handle it? Was it worth it?" For me, the answer to her questions was an unequivocal, "yes."

Student Journal 6: I am 17 years old. I live in Center City, come from an affluent family, and go to the William Penn Charter School. This winter I started two different service projects: I tutored children at the Lingelbach school, and I became involved in the Greater Philadelphia High School Partnership, which is affiliated with the University of Pennsylvania.

At the time I had no idea what lay ahead. All I remember is being uncontrollably nervous; I could not sit still on the bus ride over. I arrived with many questions: Was I going to be able to handle it? Would I make a difference in anyone's life? Would I enjoy myself? And was it worth it? Luckily, the answer to all of these questions was yes. After my first few weeks of doing community service, I was hooked. I loved the feeling I felt after I had helped someone.

At Lingelbach, I was shocked to find how many children were not at their age-level in many subjects. Nor was the school in very good condition. The Philadelphia Partnership involved the rehabilitation of the Vare Recreation Center in South Philadelphia. It was, when I began, a graffiti covered building. In both cases, the playgrounds were unsafe and run-down, and neither had a very good heating system. I also learned how understaffed each place was. If other students and myself did not volunteer, many of the improvements might not have happened.

These two experiences center on the culture of poverty that exists in the City of Philadelphia. Many people are neglected and, even worse, they are not given a fair chance to make a better life for themselves. If Mayor Rendell offered me unlimited resources to address a major need in Philadelphia, I would want to use these resources to solve the problem of neglect.

I would want to make it possible for there to be more than enough teachers in the Philadelphia public schools. They would have to be the kind of people who can nurture self-esteem in children. These teachers would care about their students' feelings, education, and success. I also would want to make sure that children were given the supplies they need. Overall, I would want to enhance the atmosphere and buildings the children come to learn and play in.

The improvements I suggested are only small steps in solving the problem of neglect that exists in Philadelphia. I believe that if every person helps a little, then in the end this problem may not exist anymore. People, especially students, must realize that everyone can make a difference. All it takes is the desire to help someone, and a heart that cares for others.[11]

Service learning in the history curriculum can take many forms. I have also introduced my students to: a citizenship project that resulted in a community needs assessment presented to local government; an intergenerational oral history project that provided both students and senior citizens the opportunity to work together in writing local history as well as creating a mutual understanding of one another; internships at Independence National Historical Park and local historical societies that allow students to gain hands-on experience in such fields as museum studies, preservation, and historical research while also contributing to the needs of those institutions; and individual local history research papers that, after extensive revision, are donated to the archives of the local institution that provided the subject matter and research materials for the students.[12]

Summary

All of these projects are tied to some form of writing because of the need for thoughtful reflection. The act of writing a script for a living history play or keeping a journal allows the student to think critically about the exercise and to develop his or her thoughts from a concrete or descriptive form to a more meaningful and abstract interpretation of the activity. In each case, the writing process also allows the student to personalize history, and to understand that there are no "right" or "wrong" answers when it comes to their own family's history, but rather that history, especially family history, is interpretation that can often give meaning and direction to those who take the time to explore it. More important, living history, simulation exercises, and service learning demonstrate to students the practical and enjoyable application of a discipline which has, for too long, been criticized for a lack of creativity and relevance to contemporary life.

Endnotes

1. Roy Rosenzweig and David Thelen, *The Presence of the Past: The Meaning of History in American Life* (New York: Columbia University Press, 1998).

2. For more on living history see Jay Anderson, *The Living History Source Book.* (Nashville, TV: American Association for State and Local History, 1985); Anderson, *Time Machines: The World of Living History.* (Nashville, TN: American Association for State and Local History, 1984); and National Association for the Preservation and Perpetuation of Storytelling, P.O. Box 309, Jonesborough, TN 37659.

3. The Federal Convention simulation I created was based on the following models: "1787: A Simulation Game." (Olcott Forward, a Division of Educational Audio Visual Inc., 1981); "Miracle at Philadelphia: The Constitutional Convention." (Independence National Historical Park, 1986); and "This Constitution: Our Enduring Legacy." (American Historical Association & Congressional Quarterly, 1986).

4. For more information about delegates, see Catherine Drinker Bowen, *Miracle at Philadelphia: The Story of the Constitutional Convention* (Boston: Little, Brown & Co., 1966); Christopher Collier and James L. Collier, *Decision in Philadelphia: The Constitutional Convention of 1787.* (New York: Random House, 1986); Robert G. Ferris and James H. Charleton, *The Signers of the Constitution.* (Arlington, VA: Interpretive Publications, 1986); and James Madison, *Notes of the Debates in the Federal Convention of 1787.* (Athens, OH: Ohio University Press, 1985).

5. Service learning is quickly becoming a powerful, dynamic way of teaching and a meaningful philosophy for many public and private schools across the nation. Since President Bill Clinton signed the National Service Trust Act in 1993, many city and statewide service initiatives with links to graduation have been established. Among the first states to institute a service learning requirement for graduation were Maryland, New York, Vermont, and Pennsylvania. Much of the early research on service learning focuses on these programs and includes: Senator Edward M. Kennedy, "National Service and Education for Citizenship, "*Phi Delta Kappan* (June 1991): 772; Dan Conrad and Diane Hedin, "School-based Community Service: What We Know from Research and Theory," *Phi Delta Kappan* (June 1991): 743–49; Robert Serow, "Students and Voluntarism: Motives of Community Service Participants, "*American Education Research Journal* (Fall 1991): 543–56; Barbara Jacoby, "Bringing Community Service into the Curriculum," *Chronicle of Higher Education* (August 17, 1994): B2; and Joseph Kahne and Joel Westheimer, "In Service of What? The Politics of Service Learning," *Phi Delta Kappan* (May 1996): 593, 599.

6. Les Parsons, *Response Journals* (Portsmouth, NH: Heinemann, 1990). Parsons advocates a step-by-step system on how to use the journal for responding to reading and literature, media, small-group discussions as well as how to evaluate those student responses. While I do agree with his theory that structure and evaluation is necessary in journal keeping, I do not go to the same lengths of defining that structure or evaluating my students' journals.

7. Theodore Hershberg, "The Case for Regional Cooperation," *The Regionalist* (Fall 1995): 21–24.

8. Center for Greater Philadelphia, *Students' Guide to Greater Philadelphia High School Partnership*. (Philadelphia: Center for Greater Philadelphia, 1995): 1; and Neil R. Pierce, "Young people want to make a difference in their communities by volunteering," *Philadelphia Inquirer*, June 29, 1996: A10.

9. W. E. B. DuBois, *The Philadelphia Negro: A Social Study*. (Philadelphia: University of Pennsylvania, 1899, reprinted in 1996 with an introduction by Elijah Anderson); and Cornel West, *Race Matters* (Boston: Beacon, 1992). Widely considered the foremost black intellectual of the twentieth century, William Edward Burghardt DuBois was the first black to earn a doctorate from Harvard. Excluded from teaching in white American colleges, the introverted young scholar found himself an outsider looking in. When the University of Pennsylvania offered him an appointment in sociology in 1896, he seized the opportunity. But Penn had no intention of allowing DuBois in the classroom. It hired him to conduct an empirical investigation to prove the deeply ingrained notion among Philadelphia's white middle class that their "great, rich, and famous city was going to the dogs because of the crime and venality of its Negro citizens."

Over the next 18 months, DuBois lived in and studied Philadelphia's seventh Ward, where the black population was concentrated. The product of his study was *The Philadelphia Negro,* one of the first studies to integrate urban ethnography, social history, and descriptive statistics. DuBois concluded that the poverty and crime of the seventh Ward was not the result of race, but of an environment and the social conditions that confronted blacks, including the legacy of slavery, race prejudice, and job competition with white immigrants. Together with the economic depression and heated labor agitation of the 1890s, DuBois' findings made it difficult for the city's white middle class to cling to the genteel cultural standards and arrogant, self-satisfied belief in progress that characterized the Victorian era. Nor did he exonerate blacks. While DuBois asked whites for greater understanding and tolerance for this so-called "Negro problem," he faulted the city's more successful blacks for their lack of leadership. He called on this "talented tenth" to serve as leaders and role models for the larger black community before it became permanently separated from the mainstream of society.

West is widely considered to be one of DuBois' intellectual descendants. In *Race Matters,* he reassesses the relationship between Dubois' "talented tenth," or an African American elite that would serve as leaders and models for the larger black community, and its implications for the African American future. West argues that significant pockets of contemporary black Americans suffer from a collective clinical depression characterized by "horrifying meaninglessness, hopelessness and lovelessness." While he admits that the attempt by blacks to adapt to a market mentality has resulted in low self-esteem because it "attacks black intelligence and character daily in not-so-subtle ways," he does not view self-imposed segregation as the solution. Instead, he argues that "a misguided attempt to define an African identity in a white society perceived to be hostile" not only "ignores the basic humanness and Americanness of each of us," but also the "common good that undergirds the national destiny of both blacks and whites."

10. See "Farrakhan to March in Gray's Ferry," *Philadelphia Inquirer:* April 3, 1997; and "Rendell Appeals to Farrakhan for Peaceful March," *Philadelphia Inquirer:* April 7, 1997.

11. Alexis Bodenheimer, "A Young Voice on Voluntarism: Could I handle it? Was it worth it?" *The Philadelphia Inquirer,* Commentary Page: April 20, 1997.

12. These projects were promoted by the Institute for Service Learning at Philadelphia University. For more information phone: 215-951-0343. Other social studies-related service projects can be found in *Maryland's Best Practices: An Improvement Guide for School-based Service Learning,* published by the Maryland Student Service Alliance. For more information phone: 410-767-0358.

Conclusion

B y now some of you may be thinking, "But my students are not as so-phisticated as those at Penn Charter. They could never do the kind of writing that is contained in this book!" Or perhaps you might be thinking, "Kashatus is a tough grader—I wonder if he's discouraging students more than helping them!"

Take a moment to consider your own development as a writer and those teachers who influenced you. Did you have a natural inclination to write as a teenager, or did you need to be prodded? Do you consider yourself a competent writer now, or not? If you do, what teacher(s) do you credit for cultivating that skill? How did they do it?

As educators we all know that one of the most important gifts we can give to our students is to nurture a sense of self-esteem in them. When they have the confidence to challenge themselves, regardless of the subject or skill, then they will develop their own motivation. They will become their own teachers. Isn't that the very purpose of an education itself?

If you think the students at Penn Charter are sophisticated writers, its because they have had teachers who invest a lot of time and energy in teaching the skill of writing. Not all of the students are as successful as others. In this book you've read examples from students with different levels of expertise. It's true, however, that the student work in this book is taken from high school students, who have by now gone on to college. They were motivated to write realizing the importance of that skill at the undergraduate level. They practiced the skill in other classes because my colleagues emphasized the written word as well. Writing does, indeed, take practice and I make sure to give my students a lot of it, both in-class and in homework assignments. That's only half of the responsibility though. The other part depends on how a teacher assesses and grades the written work.

There is no question that I am a tough, but *fair* grader. I hold my students to a high, but not impossible standard. I operate on the assumption that the bar must be raised as the school year unfolds and I show them what I expect, both in class and in the handouts I give them (many of these you have already seen in this book). I show my pride in their successes as well as my concern for their improvement in my method of grading. Every piece of student writing has a minimum of red ink in the margins, only where it is absolutely necessary for instruction. Instead, I give my feedback in a summary comment that contains three "commendations," or praise for their work, and three "recommendations" for improvement. For position papers, I limit the commendations and recommendations to no more than two sentences. For research papers, each one takes the form of a short paragraph. The remarks may address content, style, mechanics, or my observation of improvement over a period of time. The praise is genuine, rather than praise for the sake of praise. The recommendations are constructive criticisms of how the writing can be improved. I call these "recommendations" because I hope the writer will use them as "carryovers" to the next similar piece of writing; not as a directive to rewrite the assignment or test essay.

As I've mentioned before, I just don't have the time to grade rewrites and I've found that students don't take them seriously even if I do. A student is always welcome to discuss a grade with me, but I am more interested in sitting down with them and brainstorming on how they can improve their writing. They know that I care about them, as students and as writers. Once I established that reputation in my early years of teaching, I didn't experience much difficulty with students, their parents, or administrators. I will admit, however, that writing newspaper commentary and books helps my cause. Students, parents, and administrators are more hesitant to question your grading when you are putting your own work out there for the general public to read. There are also other ways I show my students that I care.

I circulate anonymous copies of their written work in class and get them to see where a particular piece of writing has merits as well as shortcomings. I try to empathize with them by writing my own local history research paper along with them, and holding myself to the same deadlines. I try to teach humility by sharing my own work with them as well as the reviews I have received on published articles and books, both good and bad. I do this to show them that no writer ever achieves perfection; there is always room for improvement, no matter how old we are or how much education or experience we have.

Perhaps the greatest teaching tool I use, however, are portfolios, or collections of student writings over the course of an academic year. Often kept in a three-ring binder, the portfolio contains samples of student work and teacher feedback and allows students to take an active and thoughtful role in the writing process. Most writing portfolios are kept for English classes.[1] But there are similarities with those kept for history.

In both English and history the goal of compiling a portfolio is to collect evidence of the student's work in order to show how he or she has developed as a writer over a specific period of time. Not only does this build a sense of intellectual self-esteem for the students, who can see the fruits of their labor, but also emphasizes the importance of writing as a process, which must be carefully practiced and nurtured over time.

A second similarity is the emphasis on taking a flexible approach to writing. Schools today are compelled to teach a range of learning styles because of motivational, cultural, and learning differences among the students. Recent research on multiple intelligences reveals that reading and writing come most easily to those students who enjoy the ability to use words and language in many different forms. Other students find it easier to communicate through interpersonal, intrapersonal, mathematical, musical, spatial, or even bodily-kinesthetic skills. These intelligences are not mutually exclusive. To be sure, each individual possesses multiple ones in some degree. But the gifted teacher makes an earnest effort to address as many of them as possible so a student's abilities are best served. Portfolios and the activities they encourage are just one of the ways to respect student differences and provide for student success in writing.

A third and related similarity to portfolios in an English class is encouraging a personal connection so students have ownership of their work. Portfolios are not a "one-way street." They encourage ongoing communication between students and teachers in terms of compilation and assessment. Students become engaged in the process of writing and, at the end of the year when their portfolios are returned, show a special sense of pride in their achievement. For many, the completed portfolio represents one of their greatest high school achievements. Some even go on to publish writing that began as part of the portfolio.[2]

At the same time, there are significant differences between portfolios in English and history class. While there is no standard list of what a portfolio contains and portfolios may take many different forms depending on a teacher's goals, those compiled for an English course often contain photographs, record-keeping forms, and multiple revisions of a writing assignment. All of these materials reflect a student's efforts over the course of a term or, in some cases, a school year. English teachers enjoy the luxury of having their students rework the same piece of writing and therefore tend to use a *process* portfolio, showing the evolution of various forms of writing through each step, draft, and revision as well as teacher assessment and often student self-evaluation. But high school history courses are inevitably driven by content. Depending on the curriculum, a teacher may be responsible for covering all the information from the pre-Colonial period to the Cold War era by the end of the year. History teachers don't have the luxury, time, or energy to assign multiple revisions, or even to request and respond to regular student evaluations. Therefore, I have found that the *product* portfolios are more useful.

A product portfolio presents a student's best completed work at a given point in the course. I usually collect them at midterm and end of term. Because Penn Charter runs on a trimester system, that means I will review portfolios six times during the course of a school year. By the end of the year, the product portfolio collectively demonstrates the mastery of a set of writing skills. It is more than a "representative sample of writing" because the student has exercised careful thought in the selection, organization, and presentation of the portfolio. Nor does it undermine the emphasis on process. While the same piece of writing may not be reworked, the same *form* of writing is, and, in the case of the research paper, there are several skills as well as drafts that are revisited.

Another significant difference between portfolios in these two subjects involves the form of writing itself. English courses focus on many different genres: short story, literary criticism, poetry, and the reflective essay among others. In history, however, writing takes the form of an interpretation, or more specifically, an argument based on a thesis statement that is substantiated by fact and generally accepted concepts, and defended by the thoroughness of the student's own explanation.

For those unfamiliar with the writing of history, such a form may seem devoid of creativity. On the contrary, the creativity of the writing can come in many ways. The argument itself can be extremely creative if the student is willing to take the intellectual risk of challenging a traditionally accepted piece of historiography with an innovative thesis and a convincing explanation.

Creativity can also be reflected in the writing style a student chooses. While most interpretations are written in the third person, narrative form, students may be permitted to write in the first person so that they may better empathize with the historical figure or event on which they have chosen to write. Even a short story is acceptable. But again, the student must take a position and defend it with the tools of the discipline—fact, concept, and explanation.

Having said that, I ask my students to compile examples of all their written work into three sections which, like this book, are titled: "Past History," "Present History," and "Personal History." The more traditional forms of writing are contained in the first two sections, including document analyses, position papers, and the various criteria for the local history research paper. The third section is reserved for the nontraditional forms of writing such as living history plays, first-person simulations, and service learning journals. Most of the student writing samples in this book are taken from these product portfolios.

To be sure, writing portfolios take time and intellectual energy for both the teacher and the student. But they can also make a significant and meaningful difference in the history education of young people.

Those of us who teach American history can appreciate the difficulty in formulating creative lessons plans, let alone implementing a writing curriculum in our subject. But if we are to engage students in the study of history, if we are going to prepare them for their roles in a free society, then we must accept a greater responsibility for the approach we take in presenting our subject. That means instructing our students in the skills of the discipline: to think critically; to discern fact from conjecture; and to understand that not all of our society's ills have solutions, but that should not prevent us from addressing those problems. Writing, more than any other skill, can help them achieve these objectives and can lead to our own professional growth as we acquire greater longevity in teaching.

I close this book, then, by asking the very same questions that concerned me when I began my teaching career nearly two decades ago: Are we content with the quality of history education in this country? Can we, as teachers, improve our own performance in the classroom? Are we preparing our students to enter the larger society as constructive citizens? If not, then why not begin to try? The dividends will be great for ourselves, our students, and our society.

Endnotes

1. Among the best-known works on portfolios and portfolio assessment in English are: Nancie Atwell, *In the Middle: New Understandings About Writing, Reading, and Learning.* (Portsmouth, NH: Boynton / Cook, Heinemann, 1998); Donald H. Graves and Bonnie S. Sunstein, editors, *Portfolio Portraits.* (Portsmouth, NH: Heinemann, 1992); Geof Hewitt, *A Portfolio Primer: Teaching, Collecting, and Assessing Student Writing.* (Portsmouth, NH: Heinemann, 1995); Carol B. Jenkins, *Inside the Writing Portfolio. What We Need to Know to Assess Children's Writing.* (Portsmouth, NH: Heinemann, 1996); Richard Kent, *Room 109: The Promise of a Portfolio Classroom.* (Portsmouth, NH: Boynton / Cook Heinemann, 1997); and Carol Porter and Janell Cleland, *The Portfolio as a Learning Strategy.* (Portsmouth, NH: Boynton / Cook Heinemann, 1995.

2. Similarities between writing portfolios in history and English were inspired by Mark Franek, "Prospero's Lessons" (Unpublished manuscript, William Penn Charter School), 1997.

Selected Bibliography

Anderson, Jay. *Time Machines: The World of Living History.* Nashville, TN: American Association for State and Local History, 1984.

Bailyn, Bernard. *On the Teaching & Writing of History.* Hanover, NH: University Press of New England, 1994.

Becker, Howard S. and Pamela Richards, *Writing for Social Scientists. How to Start and Finish Your Thesis, Book, or Article.* Chicago: University of Chicago, 1986.

Brown, Cynthia Stokes. *Connecting with the Past. History Workshop in Middle and High Schools.* Portsmouth, NH: Heinemann, 1994.

Crabtree, Charlotte and Gary B. Nash. *National Standards for United States History.* Los Angeles: University of California / National Center for History in the Schools, 1994.

Gagnon, Paul, editor. *Historical Literacy: The Case for History in American Education.* Boston: Houghton Mifflin Company, 1989.

Gardner, Howard. *Frames of Mind: The Theory of Multiple Intelligences.* New York: Basic Books, 1993.

Maryland Student Service Alliance, *Maryland's Best Practices: An Improvement Guide for School-based Service Learning.* Baltimore: Maryland Department of Education & Maryland Student Service Alliance, 1996.

Parsons, Les. *Response Journals.* Portsmouth, NH: Heinemann, 1990.

Percoco, James A. *A Passion for the Past. Creative Teaching of U.S. History.* Portsmouth, NH: Heinemann, 1998.

Rinhart, Floyd and Marion Rinhart. *The American Daguerreotype.* Athens: University of Georgia Press, 1981.

Rosenzweig, Roy and David Thelen, *The Presence of the Past: The Meaning of History in American Life.* New York: Columbia University Press, 1998.

Turabian, Kate L. *A Manual for Writers of Term Papers, Theses, and Dissertations.* Chicago: University of Chicago, 1982.

Zinsser, William. *On Writing Well. The Classic Guide to Writing Nonfiction.* New York: HarperCollins, 1998.